CAROL SPENSER'S
STYLE
COUNSEL
petite

D1313444

CAROL SPENSER'S
STYLE
COUNSEL

petite

CLEVER IDEAS
FOR WOMEN UNDER
5ft 4in

PIATKUS

© 1998 Carol Spenser

First published in 1998 by
Judy Piatkus (Publishers) Ltd
5 Windmill Street, London, W1P 1HF

The moral right of the author has been asserted

A catalogue record for this book is available from the
British Library

ISBN 0 7499 1832 2

Illustrations by Sarah Leete
Designed and typeset by Paul Saunders

Printed and bound in Great Britain by
Mackays of Chatham PLC

Contents

Acknowledgments   6

Introduction: **Your Petite Potential**   9

1. **Your Face**   17

2. **Your Figure**   31

3. **Your Proportions**   47

4. **Your Scale**   63

5. **Your Colouring**   75

6. **Your Cosmetics**   86

7. **Your Wardrobe**   98

8. **Your Swimwear**   129

9. **Your Style**   139

10. **Ten Point Plan for Petite Style**   152

Index   154

Acknowledgments

I would like to dedicate this book to my parents, Dorothy and Edward Appleton, for making me what I am today – short and sweet, well, sometimes!

Extra special thanks to the following people:

- Judy Piatkus, Phillip Cotterell, Gill Cormode and Heather Rocklin for their enthusiasm for my *Style Counsel* books, and their exciting ideas for the future. Watch this space!

- Margaret Bateman, my secretary and personal assistant, for her outstanding ability to turn my scribble into an organised book.

- Sarah Leete, fashion illustrator, for all drawings within the book, including the humorous cartoons – what a hidden talent! (Tel: 01462 684587)

- Holbrook & Hailey, international fashion consultants, for all fashion trend analysis and forecasting. (Tel: 0171 924 4748)

- Jacky Lawson of the Petite Clothing Co., for research data and statistics on the petite market. (Tel: 01904 673873. For mail order catalogue write to: 13 Collinergate, York Y01 2BP)

- Principles Petite Collection, for Carol Spenser's outfit on the front cover. (Tel: 0171 636 8040)

- Dickins & Jones, London, for mannequin's outfit on the front cover. (Tel: 0171 734 7070)

Introduction:
Your Petite Potential

AT JUST 5ft 3in, the problems of being a petite woman are very close to my heart. Working in the fashion industry, where I am often surrounded by 6ft models at fashion shows and photographic shoots, sometimes makes me feel like Gulliver in Brobdingnag, the land of the giants. Many times I've asked to be perched on a high stool to give my fashion commentary, rather than stand next to the never-ending stream of long-legged beauties filing past me on stage.

Thankfully, we petite women are not surrounded by 'supermodels' the entire time. In fact, only 7 per cent of the UK female population is over 5ft 7in, while over 50 per cent is petite, i.e. 5ft 4in and under. So, although we may not feel it, because of our lack of inches, we petite women are the 'norm' in our society. Rather than feeling inadequate and vertically challenged, we should turn the tables and feel sorry for the beanpole models who are really genetic accidents! Women are not meant to have necks like giraffes, rib-cages like greyhounds, or legs like racehorses. If you have a short neck, short midriff and short legs, you are normal. Now doesn't that make you feel better?

Although women are gradually getting taller through the ages (my grandmother was 4ft 11in and my mother is 5ft 1in), it is still a very slow process, with only an inch or so being added every generation of 25 years. The average height of a typical adult woman (aged 16 to 64) in Great Britain at present is 5ft 3¾ in (Office of Population Censuses & Surveys, 1984). Despite this fact, the clothing industry manufactures its standard clothing to fit women of a height of 5ft 6in. This is a very odd situation, and means that petite women are being rather short-changed by the fashion industry.

DIFFERENCE BY DISTANCE

There are also distinct regional variances in the distribution of petite women throughout Great Britain and, indeed, throughout the world. As a general rule, the further north in England and into Scotland you travel, the higher proportion of petite women you find. Wales also has a higher than average distribution of petite women. Some of these variances can be attributed to diet and occupation as the North and Wales were traditionally poorer than the South which led to reduced growth. Genetically inherited racial characteristics are important too – the Celts, ancestors of the Welsh and Scots, were a notably short race.

Globally there are many races and populations who are even shorter than the British average – the Japanese, Chinese, Eurasian and Indian, for example. In Malaysia, where I frequently conduct fashion, style and colour seminars, it is a very strange experience to be several inches taller than most of the people I meet!

Some Mediterranean countries, such as France, Italy and Greece, also have relatively short populations, and where these races have emigrated to large, international cities like London or New York, this greater ethnic mix produces a higher concentration per capita of petite women. In the USA alone, the annual spend on petite clothing for women is 9 billion dollars, mostly in the large, cosmopolitan, ethnically mixed cities.

POWER PROBLEMS

When I was researching my first book in the *Style Counsel* series, I discovered a fair amount of antagonism towards the label 'petite'. In a market-research focus group, one 'short' woman (she would not want to be called petite!) thought the word conjured up a picture of 'bony little creatures with scuttling feet'. In other words, she felt it to be a patronising label which suggests weakness, helplessness and a kind of bird-like fragility. For it has to be remembered that not all short women are also skinny – a large percentage are fuller-figured (size 16 and over), and feel far from weak and helpless! What they *do* feel quite strongly is a sense of anger and frustration at the way short women are often viewed and treated in society – particularly by men.

A colleague of mine in the fashion industry, Jacky Lawson (who is ultra-petite, just nudging 4ft 10in in her stocking feet) has suffered the greatest indignity of all, having actually been patted on the head by male colleagues. Not one – but several! Like many short women, myself included, Jacky has started her own business, The Petite Clothing Co., offering *truly* petite clothing for women of 5ft 2in and under. Interest-

The greatest indignity of all

ingly, most women who make it to the top in large cor-
porations are tall and quite angular. Most short, curvy
women are not taken seriously in such male-domi-
nated environments and find it easier to strike out
alone – often taking their previous colleagues completely by surprise as they had wrongly equated lack
of stature with lack of brain power. Being short and
curvy, however, does have some benefits – you can
always use the 'little and helpless' image to charm the
bank manager when you do set out on your own...

RETAIL REALISATION

Although some women are not happy with the label
'petite' (all alternative suggestions would be gratefully
accepted), the majority of short women are thankful
that at last the high-street retailers have woken up to
the fact that petite women comprise over 50 per cent
of the population and deserve to be catered for. During the 1990s, retailers in the UK have taken the lead
from the USA and begun to design and buy ranges
which actually fit the average woman in the country.
After having spent the majority of your life pushing
up sleeves, turning over the waistbands of skirts and
taking up the hem on trousers, it comes as a complete
shock to actually try on clothes which fit in all the
right places. Eureka! All we have to do now is per-
suade the interior designers of the petite departments
and stores to lower the shelves, hanging rails, mirrors
etc so that we can actually reach the merchandise and
see ourselves in the outfits!

Since I formed my company in 1992, I have worked
with many of the leading retailers (high street and

mail order) to help design ranges suitable for petite women. Some companies who have not sought expert advice from a style and colour expert such as myself, have simply produced 'scaled-down' versions of their larger ranges and labeled them 'petite'. Although this may be the easiest and simplest option, it is definitely not the best option as far as the customer is concerned. There is a lot more to designing petite clothing than chopping an inch or two off sleeves and hemlines and using slightly smaller buttons. Yes, every petite woman wants well-fitting outfits but she also wants to know she looks her absolute best – and preferably an inch or two taller! The confidence that comes from knowing you've achieved your ultimate look can add several 'inches' to your self-esteem.

SMALL CHANGE

Petite Style Counsel will take you step-by-step through every aspect of your appearance to help you make the most of your potential and boost your stature in the eyes of others. You do not have to make drastic changes. Many of the tips and tricks outlined in this book are subtle and understated. There is nothing more obvious than a short person with a foot high hair-do and 6-inch stilettos trying to look taller. It is the combination of the right hairstyle, jewellery, neckline, shapes and colours working together which creates the perfect lengthening look for you. For another petite woman, the combination of 'right' advice may differ substantially because we are all unique individuals. No two petite women need look exactly the same.

Trying too hard!

When it comes to planning a flexible wardrobe and following fashion, *Petite Style Counsel*, will also give you options dependent on your age, lifestyle and personality. As well as having differing body shapes, figure problems and colour patterns, petite women also have different clothing needs. You may be a student, a working woman, a full-time mum or even a retired 'lady of leisure'. You may have classic, contemporary or trend-setting tastes in clothes. Throughout your lifetime your occupation, social status, income and fashion tastes may change several times. Yet, you will almost certainly remain petite throughout all these changes of circumstances and whims of fashion fancy. Petite Style Counsel will help you make the right decisions time and time again, whether shopping for a new lipstick, a outfit or a change of hairstyle.

After reading *Petite Style Counsel*, I promise you'll be walking tall forever – without resorting to platform shoes!

Carol Spenser

1
Your Face

THE FIRST RULE of style for any petite woman is: 'Keep attention focused upwards'. If you are short and the majority of people (which includes all men) are always looking down on you, it is important to keep their eyes focused as high as possible on your body. If you distract attention downwards with a brightly patterned skirt or, worse still, bright shoes or tights, this focal point of your outfit will be very close to ground level. Constantly dragging people's eye-level downwards whenever they see you, results in them coming to view you as even shorter than you actually are. Think how you feel when talking to a very tall person: the very act of tilting your head upwards towards them, adds to the impression you have of their height. Conversely, the lower you make people look on your body, the shorter you will appear to them.

Being at the top of your body, your face therefore needs to be the centre of attention and the star of the show – the place where all eyes should be focused. This is particularly important for petite business women as good eye contact is essential for effective communication and credibility. As I mentioned in the introduction, shorter women have a tougher time in the business world, but it is better to develop a credible, confident look rather than an aggressive attitude, as can easily happen.

Understanding your face shape and features is extremely liberating. It immediately helps you work out which hairstyles, necklines, jewellery shapes and glasses (if you wear them) are going to suit you best. Even hats – dreaded objects for most petite women – become easier to choose and wear when you really know what you are looking for. So let's begin by looking at your face shape.

FACE OUTLINE

At the time of writing this book I have completed nearly 9,000 style and colour analyses for women through my mail-order service (see page 158). On the application form, the one question which causes women the biggest problem is their face shape. Some women tick three boxes; some just put a huge question mark in the margin; and some, when I look at their photos, have ticked completely the opposite box! We see our own face in the mirror every day, and perhaps we become so familiar with it that we can no longer view it in an objective way. Sometimes it is easier for a friend, or a complete stranger such as myself, to accurately assess your face shape.

To work out your face outline, try to remove from your mind all ideas of what shape you think it is – difficult, but try! Remove any make-up and wrap your hair in a towel as you would if you had just washed your hair. It is best not to wear glasses as these can affect the apparent shape of your face, but if you cannot see without them you will need to leave them on! Stand at arms' length from your bathroom mirror and close one eye. Dip your finger on to wet soap and slowly trace the outline of your face on to the mirror, keeping your face perfectly still. Stand back, view the resulting shape on your mirror, comparing it with the chart on pages 20 and 21 to see which outline it is closest to – Oval, Round, Heart, Pear, Square, Rectangle, Diamond.

Your face outline determines which shapes of hairstyle will and will not suit you. Bear in mind that petite women really look best with above-the-shoulder styles or long hair worn up to keep attention focused near the face.

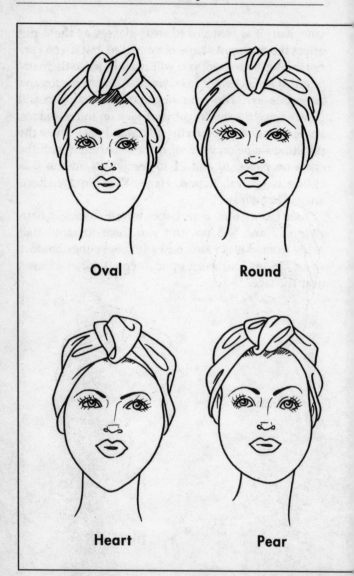

Oval

Round

Heart

Pear

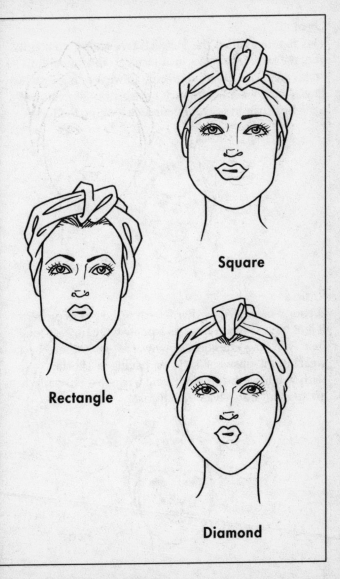

Square

Rectangle

Diamond

Oval

This is often called the 'perfect' face shape, so count yourself very lucky! An oval face can take most hairstyles well, but if you do decide to wear a 'high' style to give yourself an extra inch or two, also give yourself a slight fringe to prevent your face looking too long.

Round

A round face needs either length or height to prevent it looking too moon-like. As a petite woman, very long hair will drag attention downwards, so you are best wearing an upswept style or having a shorter style with height at the crown. Avoid a fringe – particularly an angular 'bob' style – at all costs.

Heart

Avoid a straight, heavy fringe which will make your face 'top-heavy' and turn your face shape into a triangle. A wispy fringe from a high side parting works well. You can take fullness at the chin if you wish with wedge-shaped, flicked-out or curled-under styles.

Pear

This is the opposite shape to the heart with a narrow forehead and wider jawline. A heavy fringe and fullness at the forehead work well to balance the chin. Above all, avoid fullness at the jawline – always taper the hair into the neck by the ears.

Square

The width and length of this face shape are equal, with sides and jawline all quite straight. Height at the crown is definitely needed. A spiky fringe and jagged layers at the sides will help break the square lines of the face.

Rectangle

Unlike the oval, this face shape has quite straight sides and a more angular jawline. The aim here is to give the illusion of width while also trying to reduce the length. A full fringe with an off-centre parting looks good. Short, fuller hairstyles without height on top work best of all. Centre-parted, long straight hair looks worst.

Diamond

A diamond face is quite unusual, with a narrow chin and forehead. As the cheekbones are the widest part of the face it is best to avoid fullness there and opt for fullness at the temples and chin.

FACIAL FEATURES

You may have tried to work out your face shape before, but I bet you've never ever thought about whether your features are soft or angular. Many image/style consultants only work with face shapes, but the secret of success with my make-overs – particularly with petite women for whom the face is so important – is that I also take into account *all* the facial features to ensure that glasses, jewellery, necklines, hats etc. are absolutely perfect.

So, go back to the mirror again, without the towel this time as its weight often pulls eyes and eyebrows into a 'surprised' or 'facelift' look! Study your features carefully and tick the boxes on page 26

CURVED FEATURES		**ANGULAR FEATURES**	
Eyebrows	Rounded/arched ☐	Straight/sharp	☐
Cheeks	Soft/rounded ☐	Prominent/sharp bones	☐
Eyes	Full/round ☐	Almond/tapered	☐
Nose	Full/squat ☐	Thin/straight	☐
Lips	Rounded/full ☐	Thin/straight	☐
Chin	Curved/rounded ☐	Square/straight	☐

If you ticked mainly in the left column, your features are mostly soft and curvy; if you ticked mainly on the right, your features are mostly straight and angular. If you ticked equally in both columns, your facial features have mixed lines, and you need to make a decision as to which lines you wish to emphasise to make your jewellery, necklines, glasses etc. all work together in harmony. To make this decision, use your face outline as the deciding factor. If it is a curved outline (Oval, Round, Heart, Pear), follow the 'curved' guidelines below. If it is an angular outline (Rectangle, Square, Diamond) follow the 'angular' guidelines below.

	CURVED	**ANGULAR**
Jewellery	Round, oval, swirls, hoops, knots, shells, buttons, hearts, scrolls, pear-drops, tear-drops, rounded-links, round pearls	Squares, rectangles, triangles, zig-zags, crosses, bars, trellis-work, stars, cut stones, stick-drops, flat-links, irregular pearls

table continues on page 28

Curved features

Angular features

	CURVED	ANGULAR
Necklines	Rounded collars and lapels, cowl, scoop, sweet-heart, shawl, pie-crust, bow, drape, dropped notch	Pointed collars and lapels, turtle, polo, V-neck, mandarin, wing-collar, square, slash, cross-over
Glasses	Round, oval, aviator, softened squares	Square, rectangular, cats-eye, wrap-arounds
Hats	Rounded crowns, soft fabrics, contoured brims, soft decorations, rounded hat pins	Flat crowns, stiff fabrics, straight brims, sharp decorations, angular hat pins

DON'T REPEAT YOURSELF

One word of warning, when choosing your jewellery and glasses shapes, always be careful not to repeat your face outline exactly. For example, a round face will suit oval, shell or tear-drop earrings much better than completely round ones. Similarly, a square face is better with triangular, star or stick-drop earrings rather than a square pair which completely repeat and emphasise the face shape. Similarly, round faces look good in oval glasses; square faces in rectangular frames.

You are now on the first rung of the ladder in designing your ultimate look. As a petite woman, you also, however, need to consider the scale of your jew-ellery, hats, glasses (see Chapter 4) and also which *colours* will be most flattering for all those important items around your face (see Chapters 5 and 6).

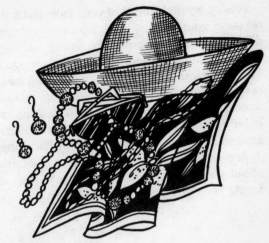

Curved accessories

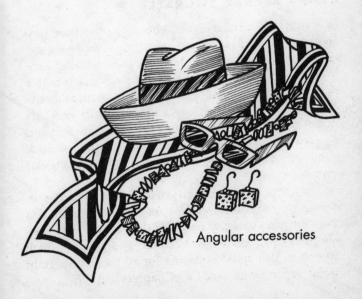

Angular accessories

Finally, on the subject of your face, you will need to reassess your outline and features throughout the different stages of your life. Some women's faces become more bony and angular as they age (e.g. Mrs Thatcher), and if you stick to a soft, full hairstyle the result can look like candy floss on a stick! Some women's faces become softer and fleshier as they get older (e.g, Hillary Clinton), and too many angles around such faces are harsh and unflattering.

Armed with these first useful pieces of information about yourself, we'll now move on to look at the differing body outlines of petite women.

2
Your Figure

BUYING CLOTHES from petite ranges is no guarantee that those clothes are going to make you look fantastic just because the measurements have been scaled down. You need to know which shapes and styles to select from the petite ranges to make the most of *your* figure as well as to make you feel comfortable. When you know you are looking good your confidence will be boosted, which in turn will help you walk taller!

If the area around your face is the most important part of your body to get right, the second most important area is definitely around the waist and midriff. Many petite women look very 'bundled-up' around their waistlines with very fitted jackets, big belts or full skirts. Not all petite women can carry off a style with such a great deal of waist emphasis as, very often, one of the reasons for petite height is a short rib-cage. This can result in a lower bustline and, sometimes, the look of a wider waistline.

Some petite women (particularly those who are fuller-figured) have no waistline at all and should avoid any kind of waist emphasis, opting for a completely straight, streamlined look to their garments. Only those petite women with small waists, longer rib-cages and high bustlines can really get away with lots of waist emphasis in their outfits.

FIGURE IT OUT

What this really means is that you have to figure out whether you are 'straight up and down', 'all in and out', or 'somewhere in between'. To do this you need to take another objective view of yourself – this time in your undies in the privacy of your bedroom. If you have a leotard and stretch belt, it is even easier to view your outline and perhaps a little more flattering than your undies! Put your arms away from your sides, keep your legs together and study the area from under your arms to your thighs to see which of the figures on the following pages you most closely resemble.

Your figure may be fatter or thinner than those shown in the illustrations. Your weight is not important when looking at the exterior silhouette of your body. Many people associate being curved with being fat, but you can be extremely curvey and slim! Conversely you can be very overweight and very straight up and down. Look carefully at your figure.

Straight Body

- Straight and/or wide rib-cage
- Little or no visible waistline
- Straight hips and thighs

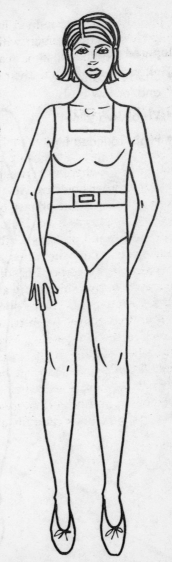

Tapered Body

- Short rib-cage and/or low bust
- Visible waistline
- High, rounded hips

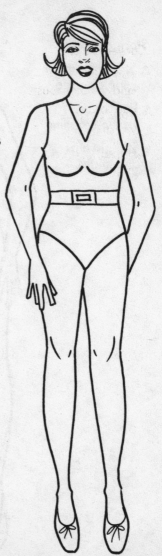

Curved Body

- Long rib-cage and/or high bust

- Very obvious waistline

- Flared hips and thighs

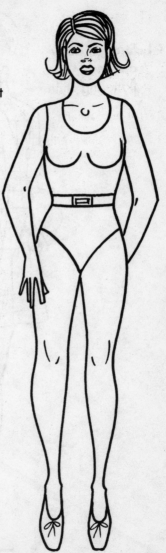

1. Straight Body
dressed in a
flattering style

1. Straight Body

Women often worry that a Straight body means one which is unfeminine. This is definitely not the case! Many of the world's most glamorous women who have become fashion icons, like Princess Diana and Jackie Onassis, had quite Straight figures with barely noticeable waistlines leading down into relatively flat hips and thighs. This figure will always look best in garments with Straight, tailored lines with little waist emphasis at all. A Straight body can be very slim or fuller-figured and when this woman puts on weight, it will generally be distributed evenly over the whole body.

When slim, the Straight figure can tuck in tops and wear belts (best belts have an angular buckle), whilst keeping the tops, trousers and skirts quite straight in design. When fuller-figured (size 16 and over), the Straight figure is best to avoid tucked-in styles belts or any kind of waist emphasis at all. Straight, single-breasted jackets, tunics, over-blouses and sweaters definitely look best over straight skirts and trousers on a fuller-figured, Straight body.

Women with a Straight body usually put on weight over their entire frame in an even way, and therefore remain straight throughout their life, regardless of their age or weight. If however, you want to create the illusion of a slimmer waist, this can be done by exercising the upper body to build up the shoulders. Broader shoulders will make your waistline look smaller by comparison. Princess Diana achieved this look very successfully in the last years of her life.

2. Tapered Body
dressed in a
flattering style

2. Tapered Body

The Tapered figure definitely has a curved outline, but because of the short rib-cage and/or low bust, too much waist emphasis can cause the body to resemble a bag of potatoes tied in the middle – not very flattering! Many petite women have short rib-cages and, as they get older, when the bust may become fuller and lower, so the ability to take a lot of waist emphasis lessens dramatically. Very fitted styles and wide belts need to be eliminated from the wardrobe.

Whether slim or fuller-figured, the most flattering styles for the Tapered figure have only gradual waist emphasis – semi-fitted jackets, blouses, dresses, coats etc. Very slim belts or wider low-slung belts can look good (look for curved belt shapes), and skirts and trousers with narrow or no waistbands work well.

When the Tapered figure puts on weight, the bust and hips become even closer together, causing the waistline to begin to disappear. If a lot of weight is put on, the Tapered figure will eventually become Straight and should follow the guidelines on the previous pages.

3. Curved Body
dressed in a
flattering style

3. Curved Body

The main difference between the Curved body and the Tapered body, is that it has a longer rib-cage and higher bust which leaves much more space around the midriff and waistline for very curved styles with features such as wide belts, peplums, fuller skirts etc. Many people associate curvy clothes with fuller figures, but you actually need to be quite slim to wear them well.

The Curved petite woman will never be flattered by very straight clothing. Because the waist and midriff area are her greatest asset, she is always best to emphasise it to give a neat, slim, trim silhouette. Straighter jackets can be worn, but look better left open to show off the waistline underneath.

When the Curved figure puts on weight, the measurements of the bust, waist and hips may increase by several inches. However, because of the long rib-cage and lower hipbones, the body has the space to take the extra weight and still remain curved. If a lot of weight is put on the Curved body may become Tapered but hardly ever becomes Straight.

GO WITH IT

Once you have identified your body outline, choosing your most flattering clothes from the petite ranges becomes so much easier. Have the style guidelines in your head and don't be tempted to stray from them 'just for a change'. Above all, don't ever buy an outfit because it looks good on another petite friend, relative or complete stranger! The reason it looks good on them is because *they* are in it. Their body may be one shape, and yours may be quite different, so although you can admire their outfit (even love it), you have to accept that it's probably not the style for you.

Your best style is therefore one which goes with and follows your basic outline rather than fights against it. Quite simply, if your body is Straight, always choose straight lines for your clothing; if your rib-cage is short or bust low, then choose clothing which gently tapers in and out at the waistline; if you dramatically go in and out, then by all means emphasise your waistline as one of your assets with very curvy styles. Whatever you do, don't try to turn yourself into someone you're not.

Many women spend their whole lives trying to look like someone else – a friend, film star or even a picture from a magazine. True style comes from accepting the shape you have been given (which is basically determined by your bone structure), and having the confidence to enhance it rather than trying to change or conceal it. So study the chart opposite to obtain a good idea of your best styles for different types of garments, then strut out in (petite) style!

FIND YOUR BEST STYLE

1. Straight Clothes

Crombie coats

Duffel coats

Straight raincoats

Straight blazers

Safari jackets

Double-breasted jackets (if slim)

Ribbed sweaters

Straight shirts

Chanel-style cardigans

Camisole tops

Straight skirts

Straight trousers

Straight jeans

Straight tunics

Tailored shorts

Shift dresses

Shirt-waister dresses

Straight pinafore dresses

Coat dresses

Column evening dresses

2. Tapered Clothes

Princess-style coats

Reefer jackets

Swing raincoats

Semi-fitted jackets

Back-belted jackets

Single-breasted jackets

Twin-sets

Fitted shirts

Fitted waistcoats

Gilets

Tapered skirts

Tapered trousers

Easy-fit jeans

Fitted tunics

Culottes

Fitted slip dresses

Empire-style dresses

Fitted pinafore dresses

Wrap-over dresses

Dipped-waist evening dresses

3. Curved Clothes

Bathrobe-style coats

Drawstring parkas

Belted trench-coats

Belted jackets

Peplum jackets

Centre-button jackets

Cropped sweaters

Tie-front shirts

Belted blouses

Bodies

Gored/flared skirts

Gathered-waist trousers

Stretch jeans

Belted tunics

Shorts (flared shorts)

Belted dresses

Two-piece dresses

Belted pinafore dresses

Tea dresses (40s style)

Skirted evening dresses

Evening dresses

Straight
(column dress)

Tapered
(dipped-waist dress)

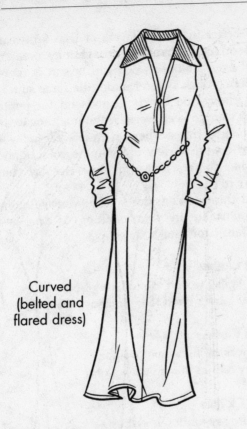

Curved
(belted and
flared dress)

FABRIC CHOICE

Petite women need to be careful about the type of fabric they choose for their clothing, as too much bulk
can turn a small person into a living Michelin Man!
Steer clear of anything, therefore, that has too much
padding (e.g. very thick quilted jackets) or too much
texture (e.g. mohair, thick bouclé, nobbly knitwear).
For warmth in winter weather, a petite woman will

look much better in several layers of thin knitwear (e.g. a twin-set) rather than one large chunky sweater. A waistcoat over a blouse worn with a suit is more flattering than a thick sweater under the same suit.

Thermal undies too can be a godsend for petite women who want to keep warm without adding extra bulk to their short frame. Thermal underwear today is produced in a wide variety of feminine colours and styles – it has come a long way since the day your granny wore it!

The final thing to consider so that you feel completely comfortable in your clothing, is the best weights of fabric for your body shape:

1. Straight Clothes
- Crisp, tightly woven fabrics work best.
- Drapey fabrics need to be in heavy weights.

2. Tapered Clothes
- Crisp fabrics in medium weights.
- Drapey fabrics in medium weights.

3. Curved Clothes
- Soft, drapey fabrics work best.
- Crisper fabrics need to be in light weights.

3

Your
Proportions

HAVING ESTABLISHED which overall silhouette you should be aiming for with your outfits, we now need to look at how you can try to elongate all the different areas of your body to create the illusion of an extra few inches to your height. By making your neck, torso and legs each look a little longer, the cumulative effect can be quite considerable. Every small detail of your outfits – pockets, patterns, seams, scarves, jewellery – can contribute to the apparent length or size of the different parts of the body they are covering.

To understand the basic principle of how to achieve this amazing feat, you need first of all to understand how the human eye is affected by the direction of any line it sees. Quite simply the eye follows a line and then automatically lengthens it to make it appear slightly longer than it actually is. Study the illustration on page 48.

Both vertical lines are *exactly* the same length, but the one on the left appears to be longer because the eye follows the outward-pointing lines beyond their

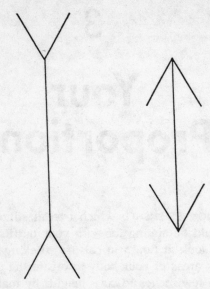

Line illusion! Which line is longer?

actual length. On the right the eye follows the vertical line but is then immediately dragged back by the inward-pointing lines making the central vertical line appear shorter. If these two vertical lines were petite women, the one on the left would look much taller – and slimmer!

The eye also follows *horizontal* lines and extends them in the same way – so if you are petite and also fuller-figured, you need to avoid horizontal lines on your outfits as these will make you look wider – and, looking wider always makes you look shorter. Darker colours and matt (not shiny) fabrics will also help reduce the size of any larger parts of your figure. Those readers who already know my views on colour analysis will know that I believe that any person can wear *any* colour on the major part of their body – as long as the style is right for them as an individual. Only the colour directly next to the face needs to be your 'right' colour (collars, scarves, make-up etc.). A fuller-figured petite woman will always look better with deeper shades for the major part of her outfit, with an accent of her 'right' shade next to her face. (See Chapter 5 for your best 'next-to-the-face' colours.)

Dressing from head to toe in one colour – monochromatic dressing – will always make you appear taller because of the strong vertical block of colour and complete absence of horizontal lines which dressing in different colours produces.

In summary, you need to remember the following eight rules to add extra inches to your height:

1. Vertical lines make you look taller.

2. Upward pointing features make you look taller.

3. Downward pointing features make you look shorter.

4. Horizontal lines make you look wider and therefore shorter.

5. Deeper colours are more slimming and therefore lengthening.

6. Matt fabrics are more slimming and therefore lengthening.

7. Lighter colours are fattening and therefore shortening.

8. Shiny fabrics are fattening and therefore shortening.

Whatever figure problems you have – double chin, big bust, large hips or short legs – can all be helped by applying these eight simple rules.

YOUR FIGURE PROBLEMS

Tick the boxes below for any figure proportions which cause you problems and which you would like to diminish. Number your figure problems in order of importance with No.1 being the most problematic for you, then follow the advice given on pages 51 – 62. Should the advice given for one problem conflict with that of another, take the advice for the concern which is most troublesome to you.

☐ Short neck/double chin

☐ Broad shoulders

☐ Narrow/sloping shoulders

☐ Large bust

☐ Flat-chested/small bust

☐ Short-waisted (short distance from bust to waist)

☐ Large hips/tum/bum/thighs

☐ Thick calves/ankles

☐ Short legs

SHORT NECK OR DOUBLE CHIN

Looks Good

- Open collars – give the illusion of a longer, slimmer neck
- V- or scoop-necklines – depending on whether your face is angular or soft
- Medium-length necklaces
- Collarless jackets worn alone
- Scarves tied loosely – don't clutter the neck area
- Shorter hairstyle

Looks Bad

- High necklines – bows, ties, pie-crust collars etc.
- Polo- and turtle-necks – these widen short necks
- Mandarin and Nehru-style collars
- Scarves tied high – this emphasises the problem
- Choker-style necklaces – which draw attention to the problem

BROAD SHOULDERS

Looks Good

- Small or no shoulder-pads – not necessary

- Raglan sleeves – the seam lessens the shoulders

- Halter-necks – great for swimsuits or dresses

- V- or scoop-necks (depending on your face) – the depth of the neckline lessens the width of your shoulders

- Thin straps on swimsuits, dresses and nighties etc.

Looks Bad

- Wide/slash necklines

- Brooches pinned wide on the shoulder

- Details at shoulder, e.g. gathers, pleats, horizontal stripes, yokes

- Large epaulettes – which make shoulders more noticeable

- Broad, wide-set straps on swimsuits, dresses, nighties etc.

- Large shoulder pads

NARROW OR SLOPING SHOULDERS

Looks Good

- Cap sleeves, which flare out from the shoulder

- Boat or slash necklines

- Horizontal details at shoulders, e.g. epaulettes/stripes

- Gathers, pleats, yokes at or near shoulders

- Shoulder-pads – angular or soft, depending on angular or soft face

- Wide-set, thick straps on swimsuits, evening dresses, sundresses, nighties etc.

- Wraps around shoulders with evening wear

Looks Bad

- Puff sleeves without shoulder pads – the height of the puff emphasises the slope

- Very low V- or scoop-necklines without shoulder pads

- Raglan sleeves – the seam emphasises the slope or narrowness

- Halter-necks – a halter also emphasises the slope or narrowness

- Brooches worn on the lapel or bust

LARGE BUST

Looks Good

- Vertical or diagonal details on top garments
- Dolman sleeves
- Plain matt fabrics on top
- Loose-fitting garments on top
- Medium-length necklaces
- Darker colours on top
- Wrap-over style tops
- Low/drop-waisted styles
- Brooches wide on shoulder

Looks Bad

- Large patterns on top
- Horizontal details across bustline
- Shiny fabrics on top
- High-waisted styles
- Brooches on lapel
- Breast pockets (particularly with buttons!)
- Tight-fitting tops
- Very long scarves and necklaces (which dangle over the precipice!)

FLAT-CHESTED/SMALL BUST

Looks Good

- Uplift/padded bra
- Horizontal lines/seams/gathers at bustline – to increase width and bulk
- Breast pockets – add detail at bustline
- More texture on top – to add substance
- Layering, e.g. cropped waistcoats over shirt

Looks Bad

- Very low neckline – shows lack of cleavage
- High-waisted styles – draws attention up to bust level
- Tank-style swimsuits – support ones are better
- Vertical stripes on top – have unwanted slimming effect
- Very tight top (e.g. bodies) – shows what you have not got!

SHORT-WAISTED

Looks Good

• Thin belts

• Belts in the same colour as top garment

• Garments without waistband

• Uplift bra to lengthen midriff

• Blouses worn outside or 'bloused-out' over bottom garment

Looks Bad

• Contrasting belts

• Top garments tucked in tightly

• Wide belts and cummerbunds

• Poorly fitting bra giving low bust

• High-waisted styles of skirts and trousers

LARGE HIPS/TUM/BUM/THIGHS

Looks Good

- Longer-style plain shorts
- Vertical stripes and seams on bottom garments
- Solid deep colours on bottom half
- Matt fabrics on bottom half
- Prints, lighter or brighter colours on top
- Control briefs and tights
- Stitched-down pleats and eased waistbands
- Scarves, jewellery to draw attention upwards
- Shoulder-pads (if necessary) or horizontal detail on shoulders to balance bottom half

Looks Bad

- Horizontal details on lower half
- Jackets/tops ending across widest point
- Very short skirts and shorts
- Light or shiny fabrics below the waist
- Back vents in jackets
- Prints or patterned skirts, trousers, leggings
- Pockets on lower garments
- Gathered ankles
- Long, dangly shoulder bags
- Tightly fitting lower garments (beware VPL – Visible Panty Line!)

THICK CALVES/ANKLES

Looks Good

- Knee, or below-knee-length skirts
- Deeper, matt hosiery
- Stirrup trousers
- Darker coloured shoes and boots
- Flat, broadly strapped sandals
- Substantial soles and heels
- Toning tights and shoes
- Knee-length boots

Looks Bad

- Pale, shiny tights
- Thin spindly heels
- Calf-length trousers or Capri pants
- Calf-length skirts
- Leggings
- Delicate strappy shoes and sandals
- Calf-length or ankle boots (unless tights match boots)

SHORT LEGS

Looks Good

- Shorter skirts
- High-waisted skirts and trousers
- Cropped trousers (e.g. Capri pants)
- Tights to match shoes and hemline
- Medium heels
- Vertical designs on skirts/trousers
- Slim trousers

Looks Bad

- Border designs at hemline
- Long, full skirts
- Turn-ups on trousers
- Gathered ankles
- Very high or very flat shoes
- Check or plaid skirts/trousers
- Very wide trousers

WRONG – this petite figure looks overpowered. Can you spot the six mistakes?

RIGHT – the same petite figure looks taller and slimmer with the mistakes corrected (see below)

1. Hair. 2. Neckline. 3. Stripes. 4. Skirt. 5. Bag 6. Shoes.

ASSETS NOT PROBLEMS

You may have noticed that I have not given any advice for some other proportional problems – long neck, long-waisted or slim hips/tum/bum/legs. This is because, when you are petite, these are all extremely good assets to have as they are all features which lengthen the body. Only tall women (5ft 7in and over) may regard 'giraffe necks' or 'racehorse legs' as a problem, but if you are petite and happen to be blessed with at least one lengthening feature, then definitely make the most of it!

4
Your Scale

YOU ARE NOW well on the way to establishing the best styles for your petite figure, but the final important matter we need to consider, before moving on to colour, is the scale of your body. Petite women will often be told to wear very small hats, glasses, jewellery, bags or patterns in order not to look 'swamped' or 'overpowered'. This comes back to the false assumption that all petite women are also skinny and/or small-boned – remember those elusive bony creatures with scuttling feet?

If a petite woman *is* very slim, small-boned and 'bird-like', she will definitely look better in small-scale accessories and patterns, because being surrounded by large-scale items will definitely make her look even smaller by comparison. We need to look at some optical illusions again to see why this is so. Study the two illustrations on page 64.

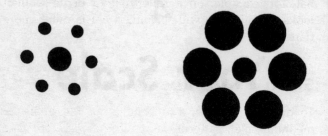

Which central blob is bigger?

The central circle in both illustrations is exactly the same size but the one surrounded by larger objects appears smaller because it is overpowered by the outer circles. If the two central circles were slim, petite women, the one with a large hairstyle, big-patterned dress, oversized glasses and jewellery, would be making herself look even smaller than she actually is.

LITTLE AND LARGE

As I mentioned in the Introduction, not all petite women are extremely thin or small-boned. Some are fuller-figured (size 16+) and many are medium- rather than small-boned. (In all the makeovers I have completed for TV, magazines, newspapers and through my 9,000+ 'mail order makeovers', I have found very few petite women who are large-boned – this is quite rare.) Those petite women who are fuller-figured or medium-boned look better with medium-scale accessories or patterns – small-scale objects will only make them look shorter and wider. A pill-box style hat, for example, on a fuller-figured petite woman looks ridiculous; a wide-brimmed hat is much more flattering.

SMALL OR MEDIUM SCALE?

To discover whether you should opt for small- or medium-scale patterns and accessories, try the following test which is as accurate a guide as possible. Try to make the thumb and little finger on your right hand meet around the wrist of your left hand in front of your wrist bone. If they do meet you are slim/small-boned. If you can only make your thumb and ring finger meet around your left wrist, you are fuller-figured/medium boned. (If you are left-handed, use the opposite hands for the test.) Shoe size can also be a good indication of bone size – not all petite woman have small feet (i.e. size 3/35 and under); many have average to large feet (i.e. size 4/36 and over).

BREAKING RULES

If you want to break the rule of scale and occasionally make a fashion statement with something quite large and eye-catching, then by all means do! Just make sure that you do it in a measured way with one large piece – a big hat, bold earrings, a huge pendant – rather than all three together, which is what gives the 'overpowering' effect. If you like to follow fashion, or have an extrovert personality, or work in a creative environment, it would not be right to confine yourself to unobtrusive accessories simply because you are

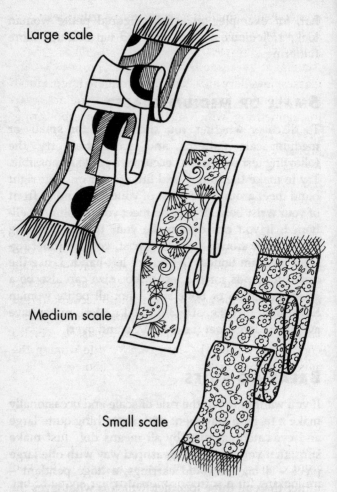

Large scale

Medium scale

Small scale

Large-scale patterns can be very overpowering on petite women. Opt instead for medium-scale if you are medium-boned, or small-scale if you are small-boned or very slim petite. Being small does not necessarily mean you have to be boring!

I would, however, recommend that you keep your 'statement' pieces to the top half of your body – hats, glasses, jewellery etc. – as it is even more important to keep attention focused upwards when you are wearing something which is potentially overpowering. A large hat for a wedding, for example, worn with ordinary shoes, is more stylish on a petite woman than a small hat worn with large platform shoes. Similarly, a large clutch bag held under the arm looks better than a large shoulder bag dangling at hip level. A large, eye-catching pendant worn with a slim belt is more flattering for a petite woman than vice-versa.

Once you have decided whether you are best opting for small or medium scale (with maybe the odd flamboyant gesture on occasions!), there are some further considerations of size to take into account to find the perfect pieces for your individual size and shape. This is particularly true for hats and glasses, which I know from my postbag can cause petite women the most agonising problems in terms of choice.

FIVE POINT PLAN FOR HATS

1. Shape-up
From Chapter 1, you should now know whether you are looking for a softer or more angular shape of hat dependent on your face shape and facial features. Remember to take fabric and decoration into account too.

Beware! An
oversized hat
can turn you into
a lamp standard

2. Full-length View

It is extremely important when choosing a hat to see yourself in a full-length mirror to gauge the scale of the hat in relation to your full body. If you are petite and slim/small-boned, you will then see immediately how an over-large hat can make you look like a lamp standard! Petite women should never have a hat brim wider than their shoulders. Conversely, a petite but fuller-figured woman can see how a very small hat can instantly turn her into a Stan Laurel. If the hat department only has a head and shoulders mirror, take your choice of hats to the dress department for a better full-length view.

3. Fit for Anything

Apart from some decorative fashion hats which perform a precarious balancing act, most practical, everyday hats should wedge firmly on the head and be in no danger of blowing away with the first puff of wind. If a hat fits properly, you should be able to feel the top of your head in the top of the crown; the hat should not fall off if you put your head upside down; and the sides or the crown should not be wider than the sides of your face. Hat pins can be used to secure a hat to your hair, but today these are more decorative than practical.

4. Hairstyle Dilemma

You should always consider how you will be wearing your hair when choosing a hat, as this can affect the best style and sometimes the fit. When you are petite, it is usually better not to have long hair showing beneath a hat as this can have the 'dragging-down' effect as well as being overpowering. Long hair (past shoulder length) looks more stylish worn up (in which case, you may need a larger size of hat) or tied back. On the whole, a short (above shoulder-length), neat style looks better.

5. Perfect Posture

A hat worn correctly can make a petite woman look taller. Many woman wear their hats very gingerly on the back of the head - rather like a halo! Even though you are short, you should pull the hat right down to your eyebrows until you can only see your feet. This means, in order to see where you are going, you need to really lift your head, which in turn elongates your neck, pushes back your shoulders and magically adds several inches to your height. Petite women often assume a hat is a very 'shortening' accessory to wear, but the right hat worn correctly is a boost to both stature and confidence. (For your best hat colours see Chapter 5.)

FIVE POINT PLAN FOR PERFECT GLASSES

1. Shape-up

From Chapter 1, you should already know whether you are looking for more angular or curved shapes for your glasses dependent on your face shape and facial features.   Remember not to repeat your exact face shape in the frame of your glasses.

2. Fantastic Fit

Most petite women have glasses which are far too big for their face – the unforgettable 'Joe 90' look! It really

The 'Joe 90' look

is quite simple to find the perfect size of glasses if you use your own bone structure as a guideline. Firstly, the top of the frame should not sit above your eyebrows; secondly, the sides of the frame should not extend beyond the sides of your face; and thirdly, the bottom of the frame should not be touching your cheeks. Frames which are too high give you a 'double-eyebrow' look of constant surprise and frames which are too low can make your nose look short and squat!

3. Weighty Problems

Glasses which are too heavy can completely dominate your face and be distracting and disruptive to effective communication which is largely conducted at eye-level. (The wrong colour of glasses for your colouring can also have this effect – see Chapter 5 for your best frame colours.) If you are slim/small-boned, delicate metal-framed or even 'frameless' glasses look best. Thick plastic frames work better for fuller faces or those who are slightly bigger-boned. Spectacle chains and cords, which go in and out of fashion, should also be considered if you choose to wear them. A thin, delicate chain for the small-boned/slim woman; a thicker leather or fabric cord for the fuller-figured or bigger-boned woman.

4. Nose Jobs

Believe it or not, glasses can lengthen or shorten your nose! A high bridge will make a short, squat nose look longer and slimmer while a low bridge will shorten a long, thin or 'aquiline' nose.

5. Eye to Eye

A dark or heavy bridge gives the illusion of bringing together wide-set (e.g. Oriental) eyes, while a light or transparent bridge will help create space between eyes which are very close-set.

FOOT NOTE ON SCALE

One final word on scale needs to be mentioned and this is on the subject of shoes. An otherwise fantastic

Mops in buckets!

outfit can be ruined by the wrong scale of footwear. Although heavy, clumpy shoes may occasionally be in fashion, petite women should always avoid them if they have very skinny calves and ankles. The result is not flattering, rather like a couple of mops in buckets – enough said!

5
Your
Colouring

MANY OF YOU reading this book may have experienced a colour analysis session and been advised on exactly which colours do and do not suit your colouring. You may, as a result of such a session, have gone home and had to clear out half your wardrobe! You may have subsequently spent hours wandering the shops on your shopping trips trying to find the exact shades in your swatch wallet – many of which may not even be fashionable at the moment.

You may be relieved to know that the colour analysis industry is no longer so rigid and that it has made developments which acknowledge the fact that today's busy woman does not have the time to be a slave to a swatch wallet! Also, the modern woman wants to be an individual with her own tastes in colours, and, if she so pleases, able to follow fashion colours each season regardless of her age. As a petite woman, you may also have found that certain colours are more lengthening (e.g. deep shades), but these may not be in your swatch wallet.

If in the past you have been analysed as a seasonal type – Spring, Summer, Autumn, Winter or even a combination of these seasons – you can now relax those rules and follow much simpler guidelines which have been pioneered by myself and other international leaders in the colour and style consulting industry.

COLOUR DIRECTIONS

The seasonal system is quite complicated – which is why you probably need a swatch wallet when you go shopping. If you are a 'Winter', for example, you need to find colours which are deep, bright and cool – a very difficult concept for the average, busy woman to hold in her head. With the system I have helped pioneer, you simply need to know which one of those three words is the most important for your colouring. If, for example, the most important word is Bright, you simply put that word in front of the name of any colour – bright blue, bright red or bright green – and those are your best colours. No need for a swatch wallet! It is very easy to remember and is a system which will work in all fashion seasons, with constantly changing colours.

I call this system 'Colour Directions' as it simply describes the main direction of your colouring from the six words which can be used to describe colours – Deep, Light, Bright, Muted, Warm, Cool. It is also a useful description because your colouring can 'change direction' as you get older or if you decide to change the direction yourself by colouring your hair, tanning your skin, wearing coloured contact lenses etc. Not many women like to remain as nature intended.

FACE FACTS

The final way in which the seasonal system has been developed and simplified is that with the new Colour Direction method, only the colour directly near the face is important. I believe, for instance that any woman can wear black – in fact, a head-to-toe black trouser suit for a petite woman is extremely lengthening. All you need to do is wear a good colour from your Colour Direction next to your face to link the black to your own colouring. Colour Direction analysis therefore only gives colour recommendations for items directly next to the face – shirts, blouses, T-shirts, scarves, glasses etc. Having the right colours next to and on your face is even more important for petite woman for, as mentioned in the Introduction, focusing attention around the face is extremely important.

Study the following pages to determine your own Colour Direction.

Deep Direction

(e.g. Cher, Paloma Picasso, Oprah Winfrey)

This colour pattern is the most common throughout the world particularly in southern climes, and is often described as *strong, powerful or dark*. If you have been made a Season, it is probably a Winter or an Autumn. Your colouring may be a mixture of warm and cool elements.

- **Hair colours:** Black, dark to mid-brown, chestnut (not red)

- **Eye colours:** Dark brown, deep hazel, olive green, navy blue

- **Skin tone:** Medium to dark (often tans easily).

- **Best colours near face:** Rich purple, forest green, burgundy, royal blue etc

- **Best neutrals:** Black, charcoal grey, dark brown, deep navy (good colours for leather accessories)

- **Best white:** Pure white

- **How to wear black:** On its own looks great!

- **Best fashion colours each season:** Any deep, strong, intense colours will suit you well

- **Best glasses:** Deep brown, grey, black, tortoise-shell, dark metals

- **Best jewellery:** Dark wooden beads, deep enamels, black pearls, shiny metals, deep stones

- **Worst colours near face:** Light, pale, pastel shades, e.g. powder pink, baby blue, beige, cream, lemon etc. Always team these with a *deeper* shade near the face

Light Direction

(e.g. Princess Diana, Kylie Minogue, Goldie Hawn)

This colour pattern is very common in Western countries, particularly England and Scandinavia, and is often described as *fair, delicate or soft*. If you have been made a Season, it is possibly a Summer or Spring.

Your colouring may well be a mixture of warm and cool elements.

- **Hair colours:** Golden blonde, ash blonde, light brown/mousey, yellow grey

- **Eye colours:** Blue, green, grey, blue/grey, green/blue

- **Skin tone:** Medium to light (often does not tan easily)

- **Best colours near face:** Pale pink, denim blue, mint green, lavender

- **Best neutrals:** Dove grey, light brown, taupe, beige, light navy (good colours for leather accessories)

- **Best white:** Ivory. (Pure white is a deep colour and will only look good if you are tanned)

- **How to wear black:** With a lighter colour or light jewellery near the face

- **Best fashion colours each season:** Any light, delicate, soft colours will suit you well

- **Best glasses:** Light framed – cream, taupe, pale grey, light metals

- **Best jewellery:** Light woods, light enamels, creamy pearls, brushed metals, light stones

- **Worst colours near face:** Deep, strong, dark ones, e.g. burgundy, aubergine, black, bottle green, deep purple etc. Always team these with a *lighter* shade near the face

Bright Direction

(e.g. Liz Hurley, Joan Collins, Princess Caroline)

This colour pattern, which is characterised by a great contrast between hair, skin and eyes, is very Celtic in origin, and is often described as *sharp, vivid and clear.* If you have been made a Season, it is probably a Winter or Spring. Your colouring may well be a mixture of warm and cool elements.

- **Hair colours:** Black, medium to dark brown, chestnut. Can be grey or blonde if brows are dark

- **Eye colours:** Bright blue, green, turquoise, bright hazel, violet (jewel like)

- **Skin tone:** Light to medium (may tan or burn)

- **Best colours near face:** Bright pink, emerald green, poppy red, peacock blue

- **Best neutrals:** Black, bright navy, charcoal grey, medium brown (good colours for leather accessories)

- **Best white:** With a tan - pure white. Pale skinned - off white

- **How to wear black:** With a bright colour or bright, shiny jewellery near the face

- **Best fashion colours each season:** Any bright, clear, vivid, sharp colours will suit you well

- **Best glasses:** Deep or bright frames, shiny metals

- **Best jewellery:** Polished woods, shiny enamels, white pearls, shiny metals, bright stones

- **Worst colours near face:** Soft, dusky, muted shades, e.g. beige, sage green, dusky rose, mustard, powder blue. Always team these with a brighter shade near the face.

Muted Direction

(e.g. Cindy Crawford, Esther Rantzen, Jemima Goldsmith)

This colour pattern is quite unusual and does not occur very frequently in natural colour patterns. It is characterised by lightish hair with darker eyes and is often described as *soft, rich or blended*. If you have been made a Season, it is probably a Summer or Autumn. Your colouring may well be a mixture of warm and cool elements.

- **Hair colours:** Blonde, light brown/mousey, yellow grey

- **Eye colours:** Brown, hazel, olive green, greeny/grey

- **Skin tone:** Medium to deep (may tan or burn)

- **Best colours near face:** Dusty rose, sage green, Air Force blue, aubergine

- **Best neutrals:** Soft grey, greyed navy, taupe, camel, (good colours for leather accessories)

- **Best white:** Oyster white

- **How to wear black:** With a muted colour or brushed, matt jewellery near the face

- **Best fashion colours each season:** Any muted, soft, rich blended colours will suit you well

- **Best glasses:** Beige, brown, soft grey, dusky pastels, brushed metals

- **Best jewellery:** Mixed woods, muted enamels, creamy pearls, brushed metals, muted stones

- **Worst colours near face:** Sharp, bright, clear colours, e.g. fuchsia pink, pure white, emerald green, scarlet etc. Always team these with a muted shade near the face

Warm Direction

(e.g. Duchess of York, Rula Lenska, Nicole Kidman)

This *golden, burnished and fiery* colour pattern is often associated with northern countries – particularly Scotland – and is characterised by an abundance of the pigment carotene in hair, eyes and often on the skin as freckles. If you have been made a Season, it is probably Spring or Autumn, and you probably have little evidence of cool elements in your colouring (unless you have dyed your hair red).

- **Hair colours:** Red, auburn, copper, ginger

- **Eye colours:** Brown, hazel, bright blue/turquoise, green

- **Skin tone:** Golden or very pale (often burns easily and may have freckles)

- **Best colours near face:** Tomato red, turquoise, apple green, peach, coral.

- **Best neutrals:** Brown, camel, tan, marine navy, rust, terracotta (good colours for leather accessories)

- **Best white:** Creamy white

- **How to wear black:** With a warm colour or gold jewellery near the face

- **Best fashion colours each season:** Any warm, golden, fiery or burnished colours will suit you well

- **Best glasses:** Brown, tortoiseshell, beige, golden metals

- **Best jewellery:** All wooden pieces, warm enamels, creamy pearls, silver with warm stones

- **Worst colours near face:** Cool, icy or bluey colours, e.g. white, ice blue, pale pink, fuchsia, grey. Always team these with a warmer shade near the face

Cool Direction

(e.g. Queen Elizabeth, Germaine Greer, Barbara Bush)

This *silvery, icy, ashy* colour pattern is often associated with older women who have gone grey – although you can, of course, go grey at quite a young age. Some brown/mousey-haired colour patterns have so little warmth in their colouring that they also fall mostly in the Cool Direction. If you have been made a Season, it is probably a Summer or Winter.

- **Hair colours:** White, steely grey, ash/mousey brown.

- **Eye colours:** Blue, blue/grey, greyish brown

- **Skin tone:** Pale, rosy or ashy (very few freckles). Can be deeper if brown eyed.

- **Best colours near face:** Royal blue, cerise, bluey-greens, icy lilac, blood red

- **Best neutrals:** Any grey, any navy, rose brown, mink, black

- **Best white:** Pure white (if deep complexion) or soft white

- **How to wear black:** Looks good on its own if you have a deep complexion and dark eyes. Otherwise wear it with a cool colour or silver jewellery near the face

- **Best fashion colours each season:** Any cool, icy or bluey colours will suit you well

- **Best glasses:** Pink, blue, silver grey and gunmetal

- **Best jewellery:** Wood mixed with silver, black and white pearls, silver, platinum, cool stones

- **Worst colours near face:** Warm, golden or yellowy colours, e.g. orange, lime green, egg yellow, tan. Always team these with a cooler shade near the face

UNIVERSAL COLOURS

There are six colours, called Universal Colours, which cannot be classed as Deep, Light, Bright, Muted, Warm or Cool. They are not particularly Deep or Light, as their strength is medium; they are not particularly Bright or Muted, but somewhere in between; and they all contain amounts of blue and yellow, making them a mixture of Warm and Cool. Because of these qualities, the Universal Colours are very 'safe' colours and suit all colour patterns either next to the face or as a complete outfit. For this reason they make good colours for bridesmaids' dresses.

The six universal colours are:

- Watermelon red – a medium, pinky shade of red

- Turquoise – a medium shade of blue/green

- Periwinkle – a medium shade of blue/violet

- Teal – a deeper blue/green (like a duck's neck!)

- Maize – a medium, greyish shade of yellow

- Coral – a medium shade of warm pink

6
Your
Cosmetics

A recent survey has shown that women who wear make-up are viewed as more authoritative and professional; are promoted over those who don't wear make-up; and ultimately earn more money than their 'naked' colleagues! Being well-groomed and well made-up can be even more of an asset to a petite woman in a work-place where taller women are simply more prominent because of their stature.

The survey did, however, state that the make-up should be 'a moderate amount, expertly applied'. In other words, too much or amateurly applied make-up can give a negative impression. In some cases, inappropriate make-up can be more detrimental than no make-up at all. Rather like having too many oversized accessories, the petite woman can be overwhelmed by too much make-up. Being short, the result of heavy blusher, lipstick and/or eye-shadow can render the wearer almost doll-like. Less can definitely be more in certain circumstances.

Most cosmetic counters in the large department stores today will give free cosmetic lessons without obligation to buy their products. Some are introducing a new 'Beauty Playground' concept where, without assistance, you can sit and experiment with different products and shades to your heart's content. If you do not feel that you are very proficient with your cosmetics, or if you have never worn make-up before (usually those women who didn't have a big sister!), then study the following guidelines and have fun trying out the techniques. You may not get it right first time, but remember that practice makes perfect.

FOUNDATION COURSE

In the past, foundations were thick, heavy and oil-based, giving an almost mask-like coverage to the skin – sometimes causing rather than eliminating skin problems! Today, base products are light, water-based and full of nourishing and protective ingredients such as vitamins, sun-screens, and anti-wrinkle agents. A good foundation is now the fourth step of skin care after cleansing, toning and moisturising as well as providing the perfect 'blank canvas' for all your other 'colour' cosmetics.

The purpose of foundation is not to change the colour of your skin but to even out any blemishes, blotches or areas of skin discoloration. You therefore need to choose a foundation which is as close to your natural skin tone as possible. Dab three different shades on to your jawline and gently blend them into your skin with your finger. The one which almost disappears, in natural light, is the best shade to choose. You may need two different shades for winter and summer if your skin tone changes.

Having selected your best foundation, dot it all over

your face and then blend it outwards with your fingertips or a cosmetic sponge. Remember to also cover your lips and eyelids to provide a good base for your lipstick and eyeshadow.

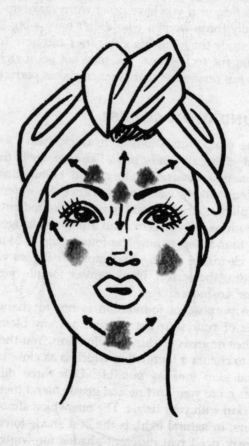

Applying foundation

CLEVER CONCEALER

Should any dark areas remain on your face, caused by deep shadows, lines or under-eye circles, a concealer is needed as an extra cover-up. This is slightly thicker and stickier than foundation and can come in a pot, crayon, bullet (like a lipstick) or a wand (like a mascara). Simply dab it on to the dark areas – usually under the eyes and next to the nose and mouth – and then blend it in gently with your fourth finger or a cotton bud.

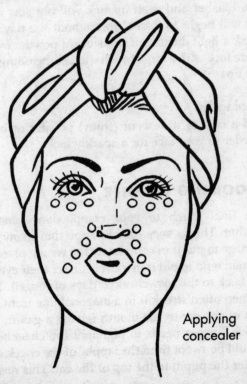

Applying
concealer

PERFECTING POWDER

Although your complexion may now look perfect with your foundation and concealer in place, it is essential to add a thin layer of translucent powder. This is not to add any more colour to your face, or even to take away the gleam of the foundation for, in the exercise-mad world in which we now live, a healthy glow can be considered an asset! Powder gives the perfect finish to the skin for the cosmetics which are to follow. Without a thin dusting of powder, your eye-shadows, blusher and even lipstick will not stay in place and will begin to 'bleed' throughout the day. Simply whisk a light dusting of translucent powder over your entire face with a large brush – again including eyelids and lips.

Evening Tip

Add a coat of iridescent (shiny) powder or bronzing powder to your face for a sparkly look.

BLOOMING BLUSHER

The final touch to your complexion comes from blusher. This is very easy to apply but many women manage to put it in completely the wrong place. Older women tend to put it in a circle under their eyes (harking back to the rosy-cheeked days of rouge!). Younger women often streak it in a diagonal line from the bottom of the ear to the mouth (giving a gaunt, skeletal look!) Blusher needs to highlight the cheekbone and should be swept from the 'apple' of the cheek (directly under the pupil) to the top of the ear. This results in a shadow occurring naturally under the cheekbone and a healthy glow on top.

Evening Tip

Whisk a lighter shade of blusher across chin, temples, nose and earlobes for a more glowing look.

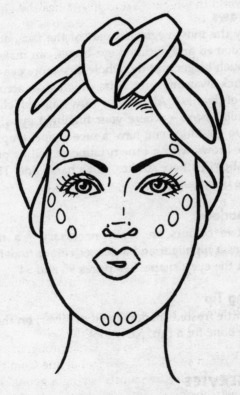

Applying blusher

MAKING EYES

The majority of women find eye make-up the most difficult. Some abandon it altogether or just resort to a quick lick of mascara or a simple strip of eyeshadow over the entire eye-lid. Eyes, particularly for petite women, are very important to get right.

Eye-brows

Usually the most neglected part of the face, and yet well-groomed and outlined eye-brows can make eyes look much bigger and the whole face more eye-catching. Pluck away any stray hairs which grow across the bridge of the nose. Also remove any hairs which cover the orbital bone – where your highlight eye-shadow needs to go. Once you have a nice shape, emphasise the eye-brows with a brown/taupe pencil or powder using short feathery strokes, not a harsh line. The difference is amazing!

Eye-shadows

Only two colours are really necessary – a neutral shade as a highlight and a deeper colour to define or correct the eye's shape. See pages 93 and 94.

Evening Tip

Try a little frosted shadow (gold or silver) on the orbital bone for a fun, party look.

LIP SERVICE

The majority of women wear lipstick as it is the easiest and quickest cosmetic to apply and also has the

Applying eye-shadow

Close-set Eyes Draw the eyes apart with the lighter shadow near the nose and the darker shadow at the outside edges. Use eye-pencil on the outer edges of the eye only.

Wide-set Eyes Bring the eyes closer together with the darker shadow nearer the nose blending outwards to a lighter shadow. Use eye-pencil around the whole eye right in towards the nose.

Applying eye-shadow

Deep-set Eyes Bring the eyes forward by using just a pale shadow over the entire eye-lid. Add interest with coloured eye-pencils and mascara (not bright) and very definite eye-brows.

Protruding Eyes Make the eyes recede with a deep colour over the entire lid and a smudge of eye-shadow beneath the eye. Avoid coloured mascaras and shiny eye-shadows.

most enhancing effect on the entire face. In fact, lipstick and earrings have been assessed as the two most important factors contributing to a woman having that finished, professional, look. Luckily, both of these take minimum time to apply in the morning!

Lip-liner
Often neglected but, like foundation and powder, it will prevent your lipstick from 'bleeding' during the day. Outline the entire natural lip-line leaving the corners free where smudging can easily occur.

Lipstick
Using a lip-wand or lip-brush, fill in your entire lip area. A lip-brush will help drive the lipstick into all the creases of the lips helping the lipstick to stay on longer. If one lip is fuller, use a slightly darker shade on it, and a lighter shade on the other lip.

Evening Tip
Add a touch of clear or slightly coloured lip gloss to the centre of your bottom lip for a luscious look!

COLOUR DIRECTIONS

Now that you know all the basic techniques for perfect make-up results, check on the following charts that you have all the most flattering colours for your Colour Direction in your cosmetic bag.

Deep Direction
Eye-shadows
• icy beige highlight
• grey, navy, aubergine, moss green

Eye-liner/Mascara
- black, charcoal, navy, teal

Blusher
- deep berry, burgundy, browny red

Lips
- red, deep pinks, terracotta, rust

Light Direction

Eye-shadows
- pink, peach highlight
- taupe, grey, sage green, lilac

Eye-liner/Mascara
- brown, brown/black, soft navy

Blusher
- soft pinks, coral, peach

Lips
- pinks, coral, peach, raspberry red

Bright Direction

Eye-shadows
- icy beige highlight
- navy, charcoal, turquoise, purple

Eye-liner/Mascara
- black, charcoal, purple, teal

Blusher
- clear pink or coral

Lips
- red, bright coral, fuchsia

Muted Direction

Eye-shadows
- beige or peach highlight
- mink, grey, sage, plum

Eye-liner/Mascara
• brown, grey, soft navy
Blusher
• peach, salmon, browny pink
Lips
• toffee, beige, dusky pink, soft red

Warm Direction
Eye-shadows
• beige or peach highlight
• brown, teal, copper, green, turquoise
Eye-liner/Mascara
• brown, brown/black, teal
Blusher
• apricot, peach, nutmeg
Lips
• terracotta, salmon, coral, orange, warm red

Cool Direction
Eye-shadows
• icy beige, pink highlight
• navy, grey, lilac, plum
Eye-liner/Mascara
• black, navy, plum
Blusher
• rose pink, berry
Lips
• raspberry, rose, bluey-red, wine

NB Teal (for eyes) and coral (for lips) are universal colours which will suit all colour patterns.

7
Your
Wardrobe

NOW THAT THE difficult part of analysing your figure, face and colouring is over, we can begin the fun part – organising your wardrobe. Like most women, I'm sure that you will have far too many clothes in your wardrobe – not to mention the clothes you also have in your spare-room wardrobe, in suitcases under the bed, or in bin bags under the stairs.

NOTHING TO WEAR?

Despite the amount of money you spend on clothes, I am also sure that on many occasions you still have 'nothing to wear'. Most women, in fact, wear 20 per cent of their clothes 80 per cent of the time, and become very bored with spending the majority of their time in the same old outfits. The reason this situation arises is because many women buy an imbalance of clothes for the kind of lifestyle they lead.

Being petite, you may find that you prefer, and feel more comfortable in, a particular style of clothes – e.g. casual wear – so you are always drawn to buying bodies, T-shirts and casual trousers, and have little to wear to work. Or, being petite, you may find simple summer clothes more comfortable than thicker winter clothes which can leave you feeling 'bundled-up', so your wardrobe becomes unequally balanced between summer and winter outfits. Or your lifestyle may have changed (perhaps from being a full-time mum to being a full-time worker again) yet you are still in the habit of buying clothes for your 'old' lifestyle.

LIFESTYLE ANALYSIS

The first thing you need to do is spend a few weeks working out how many hours of your day are spent on the different activities of your lifestyle. Keep a note each day of how many waking hours are spent on working, leisure, social and sporting activities. Add up all the hours over a few weeks and roughly work out the percentage of your time spent in each

A typical lifestyle analysis

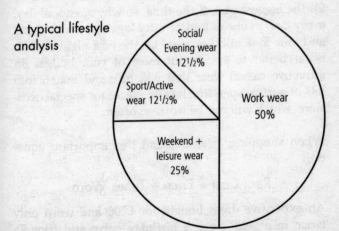

Social/
Evening wear
12¹/₂%

Sport/Active
wear 12¹/₂%

Work wear
50%

Weekend +
leisure wear
25%

category. The percentage of the different types of clothes in your wardrobe needs to reflect this lifestyle as closely as possible.

If the biggest percentage of your time is spent at work, the biggest percentage of your clothing should be work-related outfits. If you don't spend a great deal of time socialising, you don't need dozens of 'special occasion' outfits. If the majority of your time is spent at home with the children, your casual wear should be the most important aspect of your wardrobe – one pair of jeans and a few sweaters in a wardrobe of smart suits and fancy dresses is totally out of balance.

VALUE FOR MONEY

Once you know which category of clothing is the most important to your present lifestyle, you need to make sure that the major part of your clothing budget is spent in that area. You need to look and feel your best for the biggest part of the time, so why spend all day, every day, in cheap and/or tatty leggings and T-shirts and only look and feel good on the odd night out? It is far better to splash out most of your budget on attractive casual wear that will mix and match into lots of outfits, spending less on pieces for special occasions which will not be worn so often.

When shopping, bear in mind this important equation:

$$\text{Real Cost} = \text{Price} \div \text{Times Worn.}$$

An expensive dress bought for £200 and worn only twice in a year – e.g. a birthday party and friend's wedding - has cost £100 at each wearing. That £200 could have been spent on much more useful items that could have been worn in a variety of different ways, bringing their Real Cost down to just a few pounds per wearing by the end of the year. The secret of a successful wardrobe is, therefore, one which suits your lifestyle and contains quality garments which are being worn on a regular basis in a variety of different ways. Items which are hardly ever worn should be the least expensive!

WARDROBE SURGERY

Whilst keeping your 'lifestyle diary', it is also a good idea to embark on a little (or a lot) of wardrobe surgery to clear away the 'dead wood' and leave some space for your new essential and exciting purchases. This will all become clear later in this chapter.

First of all, get out all your clothes (don't forget the spare room, under the bed and stairs) and lay them on the bed – probably in a huge mountain! Now put on the floor all the items you have not worn for the past two years. The reasons you haven't worn these are probably because they are:

• Items which don't suit your current lifestyle (see above).

• Items which don't suit your petite figure (see Chapters 1 and 3).

• Items which don't flatter your proportions (see Chapter 3).

- Items which don't suit your colouring near the face (see Chapter 5).

- Items which are old-fashioned (see Chapter 9).

- Items which were shopping mistakes (pre-menstrual disasters or unwanted presents!).

Strictly speaking, you are best to get rid of these items but, as they probably comprise 50 per cent (or more) of your wardrobe, this may be difficult to do in one fell swoop. So I will allow you to store them (in the spare room, under the bed or stairs) for another year! If you don't need to go to them during that time, you definitely should banish them forever without a second thought. If some outfits were expensive, take them to 'nearly new' shops or 'dress agencies' where you can receive substantial amounts for them towards your new purchases.

PLUG THE GAPS

When you return the remaining garments to your wardrobe, the rail will no longer sag under the weight and, amazingly, you will be able to get your fingers between the coathangers – what luxury! By the way, I hope you tackled the shoe mountain in the depths of the wardrobe too...

The next step is to plug the gaps in your wardrobe by drawing up a shopping list of items you really need to make it right for your lifestyle as well as making it versatile and flexible. There are some items which all women, regardless of age or lifestyle, need to have. These are wardrobe classics which will take you any place, any time, any where:

CORE PIECES

- Navy blazer – single-breasted is best for petites

- Little black dress – knee-length is best for petites

CORE PIECES

• Raincoat – a short style is best for petites

CORE PIECES

- White cotton shirt – the 'best white' for your Colour Direction

- Cotton-knit top – with neckline to suit your face

All these pieces are so simple and timeless that they will never date and can constantly be updated with the latest fashionable accessories, shoes etc.

CLEVER CAPSULES

Once the 'core' classics have been added, you need to begin building capsules each season to ring the changes with your outfits and obtain real value for money. A capsule is simply a collection of garments based around a few colours which will mix and match into dozens of different outfits. A capsule of just 12 garments, for example, can provide over 60 outfits – so although you may have less clothes in your wardrobe, you will have ten times the amount of outfits. The 'Nothing to Wear' syndrome will be gone forever!

For your colour scheme, choose a neutral shade (black, brown, navy, grey); a lighter shade (white, ivory, lemon, pink); and a more colourful shade (red, coral, turquoise, green). Bear in mind that only the items near your face (blouses, shirts, T-shirts) need to be good for your Colour Direction. If you like the colour of a garment and the shape is great for your figure, but the shade is not the best for your Colour Direction, team it with a good scarf, blouse or jewellery or simply keep a low neckline.

If you are petite and also fuller-figured, make sure your colour scheme does not contrast too much (e.g. black, white and red) or you will be chopping yourself into distinct 'colour blocks' when you mix your garments together. Colours which blend gently together are much better.

The Versatile Capsule

A good, versatile capsule contains about 12 garments. For example:

- **A & B** – A suit in a neutral colour (e.g. brown jacket and skirt)

- **C & D** – A suit in a toning colour (e.g. coral jacket and skirt)

- **E** – A daytime shirt (e.g. cream cotton)

- **F** – A casual T-shirt/body (e.g. coral stretch-jersey)

- **G** – An evening blouse (e.g. cream satin)

- **H** – A pair of trousers (e.g. brown to match A and B)

- **I & J** – A two-piece dress (e.g. brown/coral/cream pattern)

- **K** – A knit-top (e.g. brown or cream)

- **L** – A cardigan (e.g. brown or cream)

Capsule wardrobe for a **STRAIGHT FIGURE**

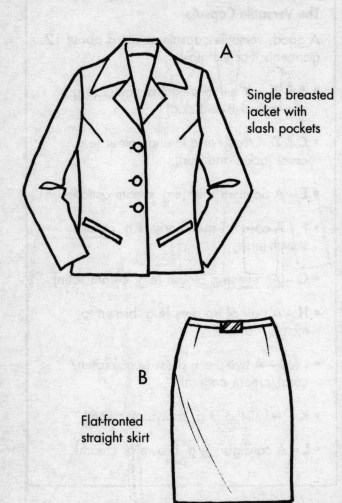

A

Single breasted
jacket with
slash pockets

B

Flat-fronted
straight skirt

Capsule wardrobe for a Straight Figure

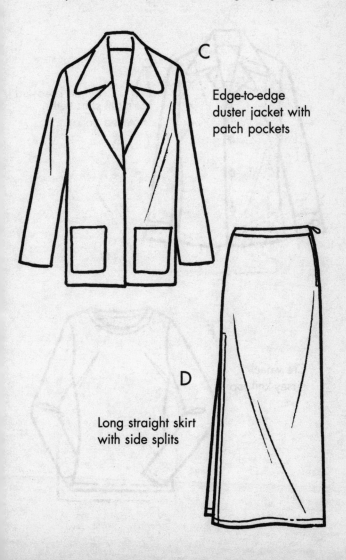

C

Edge-to-edge
duster jacket with
patch pockets

D

Long straight skirt
with side splits

Capsule wardrobe for a Straight Figure

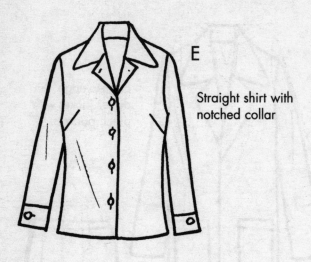

E

Straight shirt with
notched collar

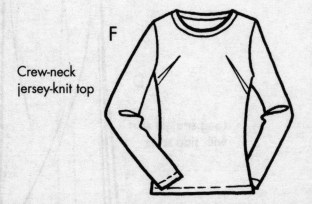

F

Crew-neck
jersey-knit top

Capsule wardrobe for a Straight Figure

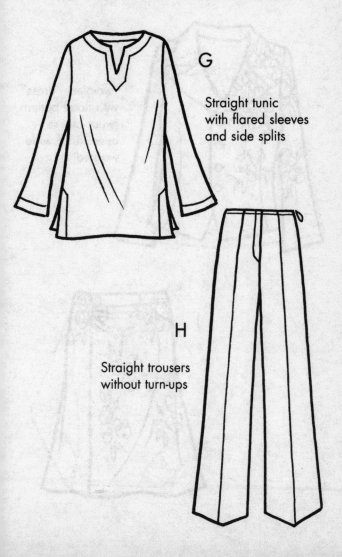

G

Straight tunic
with flared sleeves
and side splits

H

Straight trousers
without turn-ups

Capsule wardrobe for a Straight Figure

I

Two-piece 'dress' with floral pattern. (wear blouse *over* skirt if wide waisted)

J

Capsule wardrobe for a Straight Figure

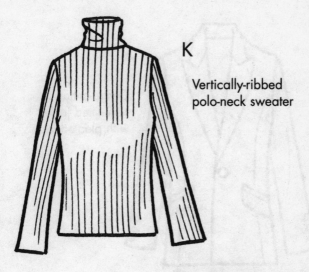

K

Vertically-ribbed
polo-neck sweater

L

Long-line cardigan
to double as extra
jacket

Capsule wardrobe for **TAPERED FIGURE**

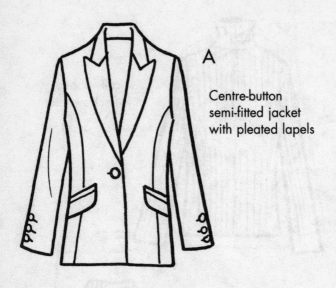

A

Centre-button
semi-fitted jacket
with pleated lapels

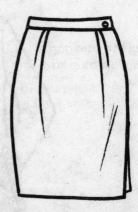

B

Tapered skirt
with front pleats

Capsule Wardrobe for a Tapered Figure

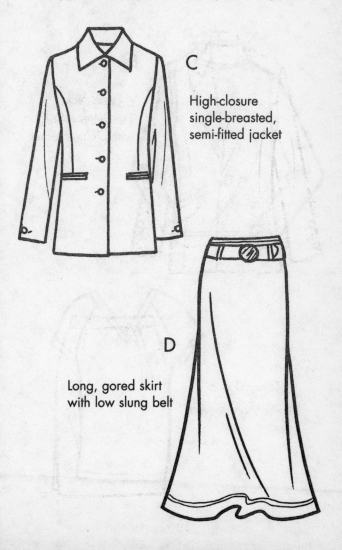

C

High-closure
single-breasted,
semi-fitted jacket

D

Long, gored skirt
with low slung belt

Capsule Wardrobe for a Tapered Figure

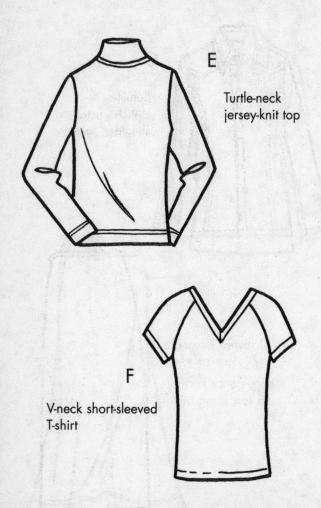

E

Turtle-neck
jersey-knit top

F

V-neck short-sleeved
T-shirt

Capsule Wardrobe for a Tapered Figure

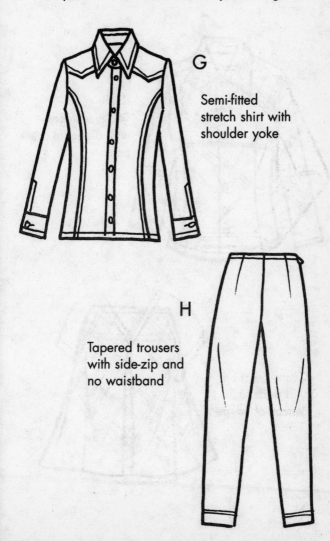

G

Semi-fitted
stretch shirt with
shoulder yoke

H

Tapered trousers
with side-zip and
no waistband

Capsule Wardrobe for a Tapered Figure

I

Two-piece dress
with diagonal-check
pattern

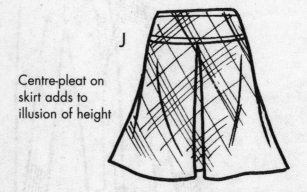

J

Centre-pleat on
skirt adds to
illusion of height

Capsule Wardrobe for a Tapered Figure

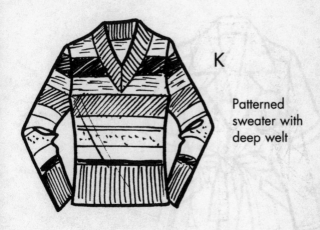

K

Patterned
sweater with
deep welt

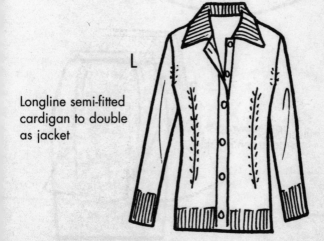

L

Longline semi-fitted
cardigan to double
as jacket

Capsule wardrobe for **CURVED FIGURE**

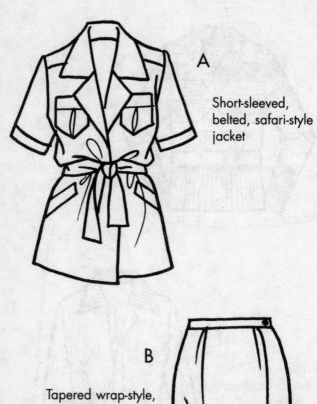

A

Short-sleeved, belted, safari-style jacket

B

Tapered wrap-style, side-fastening skirt

Capsule wardrobe for Curved Figure

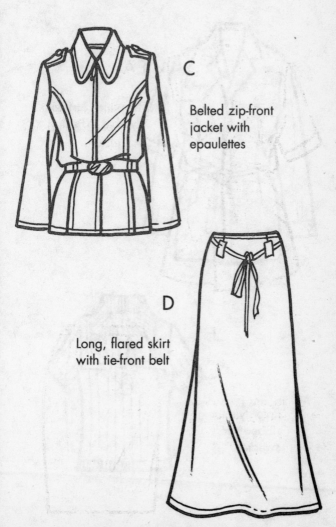

C

Belted zip-front
jacket with
epaulettes

D

Long, flared skirt
with tie-front belt

Capsule wardrobe for Curved Figure

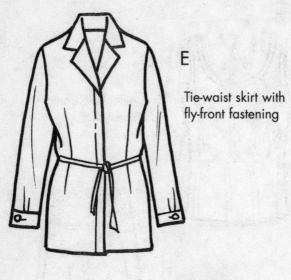

E

Tie-waist skirt with
fly-front fastening

F

Polo-style fitted,
ribbed short
sweater

Capsule wardrobe for Curved Figure

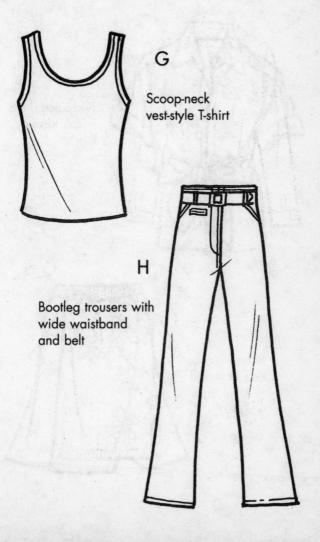

G

Scoop-neck
vest-style T-shirt

H

Bootleg trousers with
wide waistband
and belt

Capsule wardrobe for Curved Figure

I

Two-piece dress
in soft, drapey
fabric

J

Blouse can be
tied at midriff
to emphasise
waistline

Capsule wardrobe for Curved Figure

K

V-neck,
lacey-knit top

L

'Ballet-wrap'
cross-over-style
cardigan

The following combinations are possible:

1. I J	22. J E K	43. F K B
2. I J L	23. J F L	44. F K -D
3. I J K	24. J F K	45. F K H
4. I J A	25. J G L	46. F A B
5. I J C	26. J G K	47. F C D
6. I L B	27. J E A	48 F C H
7. I L D	28. J E C	49. F A H
8. I A B	29. J F A	50. G L B
9. I A D	30. J F C	51. G L D
10. I A H	31. J G A	52. G L H
11. I C D	32. J G C	53. G L H
12. I C H	33. E A B	54. G A D
13. I L H	34. E C D	55. G B C
14. I B L	35. E B C	56. G K H
15. I K B	36. E L B	57. G C H
16. I K D	37. E L D	58. G A H
17. I K H	38. E L H	59. G K D
18. E J	39. E K D	60. G H
19. F J	40. F L B	61. E K H
20. G J	41. F L D	62. E A H
21. J E L	42. F L H	63. E C H

Although 60 outfits are possible from eac
you can make even more. Wearing two o
together (e.g. a shirt over a T-shirt/body) with the
different jackets and bottoms gives additional possibilities. Don't forget that you also have your 'core'
pieces which can be integrated into the plan – the
coloured jacket over the black dress; the sweater
under the blazer etc. The possibilities become endless
and, as you add new capsules each season, they will
also soon all begin to mix together. Do remember that
the capsule wardrobes illustrated do still need to be
adapted for your face and proportions (see Chapters 1
and 3.)

Capsules, therefore, make life incredibly easy and
can be put together for any lifestyle. Obviously they
are a great boon to working women, particularly those
who travel frequently. One capsule, plus a variety of
accessories, will easily see a busy working woman
through a one-week business trip. A capsule plus a
few extras – swimsuit, shorts, sarongs etc. – will also
see you through a two-week summer holiday, easily
fitting into one suitcase. (See Chapter 8 for your best
choice of swimsuit, sarongs, etc.)

Each capsule only needs three pairs of shoes – especially for holidays – in a neutral colour to take you to
all occasions – a flat pair (e.g. loafers) for casual; a
medium heel (e.g. court shoes) for day; and a higher
heel (e.g. slingback sandals) for evening.

If you spend a great deal of time at home, don't
think of capsules as being 'too smart' for your
lifestyle. 'A suit' simply means a jacket and bottom
which match – the fabric could even be denim. The
trousers in your capsule could be chinos and the three

tops could all be T-shirts, sweatshirts or bodies etc., if your lifestyle does not require anything more dressy. In the summer, your two-piece dress for example, could be a sarong skirt with matching shirt. Your 'little black dress' could be anything from a knitted sweater dress to a spaghetti-strapped slip dress. Interpret the core and capsule idea to suit your age, lifestyle, personality and budget.

BYE BYE IMPULSE BUY!

The key to a successful dinner party lies in the fact that when you go out shopping to buy the food, you go around with a list of ingredients of the things you need. The same is true for a successful wardrobe – go around with a list of things you need when clothes shopping. If you simply go looking for 'something', you can tramp the shops forever. If you are focused on the things you need, you will find most, if not all, of them. Forget impulse buying unless you happen to see by chance something that you've been looking for or that you know will go with at least three other items in your wardrobe.

Need it badly, love it madly, or forget it – OK?

8

Your Swimwear

Trying to look a little taller on the beach or at the swimming pool is rather more difficult due to the fact, of course, that you have hardly any clothes on. You could try wearing 6-inch white stilettos like a 1960s beauty queen, but you may feel a little conspicuous! It is in swimwear, however, that you feel most vulnerable and self-conscious because of your semi-naked state, so finding the perfect swimsuit or bikini to make the most of your assets and detract from your disaster zones is essential.

Look back at Chapter 3 to see which proportional problems you ticked and in which order of importance you placed them. Then use the following guidelines to help select your most flattering swimwear.

BROAD SHOULDERS

On the whole, broad shoulders are an asset when wearing swimwear. If you feel your shoulders are too big, however, a halter-neck style with a deep V- or scoop-neckline will give the illusion of slimming them down.

Deep necklines
and halter-necks
narrow the
shoulders

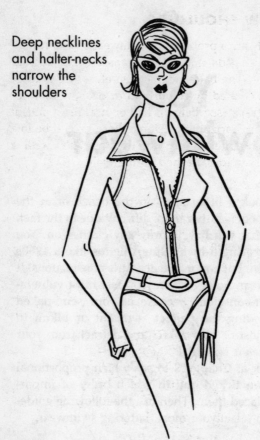

Avoid
Higher necklines, wide-set straps and any kind of details on the shoulders – e.g. bows, buttons, stripes, etc.

Sarong Advice

Tie a sarong in a halter-neck style knotted at the back of the neck to further slim the shoulders.

NARROW SHOULDERS

These really are a problem in swimwear as you cannot slip shoulder-pads under the straps to balance your bottom half! The balancing act therefore needs to be an illusion created by colour and/or design. Look for wide-set straps (see below), higher necklines and, if there are any horizontal designs, these should be in a lighter or brighter colour on the top half, with a deeper, darker, unpatterned bottom half.

Wide-set
straps broaden
the shoulders

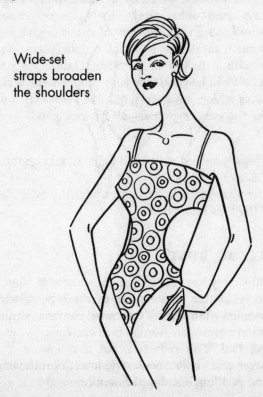

Avoid

Halter-necks, deep V-necklines, vertical lines on top half.

Sarong Advice

Tie a sarong horizontally under the arms to broaden your top half.

LARGE BUST

Being petite with a large bust can make you look very 'top-heavy' and unbalanced. Firstly, always choose underwired styles with substantial straps to give your bust as much support as possible. A dark, plain fabric on top with a lighter or patterned fabric on your bottom half will help balance your proportions. Wrap-over styles which put a diagonal line across the bust and take the eye downwards always look good.

Avoid

Thin straps, unwired suits, and light colours on top.

Sarong Advice

Never tie a sarong directly on or under the bustline – low on the hips looks best.

SMALL/NO BUST

A recent survey has shown that 13 per cent of women have an A-cup bra size – many of these being slim, petite women – but a small bust need not be a very big problem in swimwear. A small bust can easily wear an unwired, tank-style swimsuit, but if you want it to look larger and fuller choose styles with underwired cups and padding – some pads are removable to give you a choice of how much cleavage you wish to create! Twisted or bandeau-style tops, without straps, look good and also add a little more substance to the bust area. Ruffles, gathers, texture, horizontal patterns, bright colours, also have a bust-enhancing effect (see below) – particularly if the suit is plain and dark below the bustline.

Gathers and decorations enlarge the bust

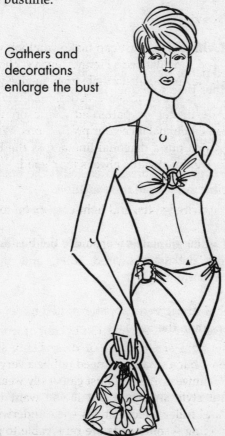

Avoid

Dark colours, vertical lines across the bust area and unwired 'tank' suits if you want your bust to look bigger.

Sarong Advice

Knot a sarong in a large knot directly on the bust to increase its size.

SHORT-WAISTED

Short-waisted petite women look better in a one-piece swimsuit rather than a bikini - unless the bikini bottom is a 'hipster' style which creates the illusion of more space between the bust and waistline. The aim is to create a longer, slimmer torso so any swimsuits with vertical lines or panels will be most flattering. Underwired cups are also essential to lift the bust as high as possible away from the waistline.

Avoid

Any kind of waist emphasis (especially belts or horizontal middle details), unwired suits, and high-waisted bikini bottoms.

Sarong Advice

Sarongs with a strong vertical pattern, tied under the arms, will lengthen the torso.

BIG HIPS/TUM/BUM

This is normally a woman's biggest concern in swimwear – trying to conceal the odd spare tyre or two! The trick is to draw the eye upwards with colour and pattern on your top half and darker, matt fabric or vertical details on the bottom half. Diagonal lines which converge inwards across the stomach and hips are also very slimming. Skirted-styles can look good but avoid these if you also have narrow shoulders as they always emphasise a pear shape. Swimsuits with tummy control panels and/or high lycra content can also help reduce inches.

Avoid

Belts, light, shiny fabrics and horizontal patterns on the bottom half.

Sarong Advice

If you have a wide waist or big stomach, always tie a sarong at an angle rather than in a straight, horizontal line around the waistline. Remember that a diagonal line is always more slimming and takes the eye downwards away from the problem area.

SHORT LEGS

A swimsuit with high-cut legs will always make short legs look longer. If you have big hips and/or thighs, however, a high-cut swimsuit can be very unflattering causing the flesh to bulge out at the sides. A medium-cut leg is therefore better, but you can create the illusion of longer legs with vertical lines on your swimsuit reaching right up to the bustline.

For short legs, mini sarongs are best

Avoid

Very low-cut leg, horizontal lines on the bottom of swimsuits and hipster-style bikini bottoms.

Sarong Advice

Avoid sarongs with border patterns which end at mid-calf, cutting the legs in two. A mini sarong or ankle-length sarong with plenty of vertical pattern is best.

FULLER FIGURE

If you are petite and also fuller-figured it is essential to have a well-fitting swimsuit – particularly one which is not too small. You will probably need a swimsuit which is one size bigger than your dress size. If you don't like the size on the label, just cut it out – no-one will know!

Fuller figures will always look better in a one-piece swimsuit in a deep, muted colour and a matt fabric. A medium-cut leg is best and built-in tummy panels give girdle-like control to your middle. Underwired cups are essential, as is a high lycra content (but not shiny). Look for plenty of vertical details (pattern, seams or panels), wide straps and a lowish neckline.

Avoid

Bikinis, thin straps, light or shiny fabric, very high or very low legs, high necklines, unwired suit, and horizontal patterns.

Sarong Advice

You may prefer alternative cover-ups to the sarong, such as sheer shirts, tunics and even light beach pants. A large sun-hat (not bigger than shoulders) will also help balance your figure.

BEACH ACCESSORIES

Sun hat – it is essential to keep the sun off your face and neck so make sure you pack a sun-hat with your swimsuits. A large brim is best if you are fuller-figured/medium boned: a smaller brim (e.g. Panama style) if you are slim/small boned. Straw hats which roll into tubes or canvas hats which fold neatly are ideal for travelling.

Scarves – light chiffon, silk or cotton scarves can serve lots of purposes on the beach. Wrap one around your head, turban-style, to keep the sun off your hair. Twist two long scarves together, knot the ends and wear around your neck to brighten up a plain swimsuit. Very large square scarves can double as a mini-sarong which are ideal for petite figures.

Bags – a large beach bag is essential to carry your towel, lotions etc. A flat, hand-held bag is better for a petite figure as it gives a more streamlined look than a bulky, drawstring shoulder bag.

Sandals – although you may want to add a little extra height to your swimsuit it is best to avoid heeled sandals or shoes. A cork or rope-soled wedge sandal or espadrille is ideal but avoid those with tie-straps if you have thick ankles.

9
Your Style

AND FINALLY... that most elusive aspect of your appearance – personal style. What is it? How do you go about developing it? Many of the letters I receive through my TV and magazine work ask these questions many times over. Some image/style/colour consultants try to answer such queries by asking you to fill in a questionnaire on your tastes, lifestyle and hobbies, which results in you being defined as 'Dramatic', 'Casual' or 'Romantic', with instructions to dress under those guidelines for all occasions.

This system, I feel, is totally inadequate for most modern woman with complicated, busy lives who need a variety of different looks for the different roles they juggle. How can you adopt a 'Casual' mode of dress if you are a bank manager? How can you look 'Romantic' all day in lace and frills looking after babies or small children? Looking 'Dramatic' in all the latest catwalk garb maybe totally impossible if you are 4ft 10in! In other words, you need to have a variety of clothes in your wardrobe to suit the life you lead. This may include casual clothes for your evenings and weekends; more romantic clothes for special occasions; and, perhaps, more sober clothes for your working life. (See Chapter 7 to make sure you have the right percentage of each category.)

FASHION PERSONALITY

What I do find, however, is that all the clothes in a woman's wardrobe – casual, dressy, working – will follow what I call a particular 'Fashion Personality'. Some women's wardrobes will be full of all the latest catwalk fashions, accessories and shoes. Some women's wardrobes will have some of the latest bits and pieces, but with a strong core of more timeless pieces. Some women's wardrobes show little evidence of the latest trends or fads, solely consisting of tried and tested classic favourites, usually of good quality to last for many seasons.

So which category do you fall into? Tick a box below:

☐ Trendy – latest looks, often extreme and exaggerated.

☐ Contemporary – current looks but not extreme.

☐ Currently Classic – timeless pieces which never change/date.

Your fashion personality can, of course, change throughout your life. You may be 'Trendy' in your teens and twenties, 'Contemporary' in your thirties, and perhaps slide into 'Classic' during your forties and fifties. It is much easier to be a trendsetter when you are younger (and usually slimmer!), but, as you get older, the ability to wear the latest fads and fashions definitely recedes. Not many mature women look good in crop tops, flares and platform shoes! Looking ridiculous, or like 'mutton dressed as lamb', becomes a big fear for women as the years advance.

FASHIONABLY CURRENT

Research has shown, however, that women who 'keep up' with fashion and look current or Contemporary appear younger and happier and, in the workplace, are viewed as having more current, up-to-date knowledge and thinking within their chosen profession than those who look outdated or old-fashioned. Many women (even those who have been trendsetters in their youth) do not know how to achieve a Contemporary look and go straight into a Classic mode of dress around the age of thirty – or after their first baby, whichever comes first! The majority of women who write to me would like to look Contemporary but don't know where to start. Even those who prefer a Classic look, need to know how to achieve a *current* classic style, rather than an outdated classic look.

CATWALK CLUES

Being Trendy is no problem – you just buy all the latest fashion magazines, copy what you see exactly and revamp your wardrobe every season. Apart from being expensive and time-consuming, wearing very trendy outfits is not always flattering to petite women as the exaggerated/extreme styles are often designed with the 6 ft supermodel in mind.

Do not, however, dismiss the catwalk pictures as completely irrelevant to you, and resign yourself to a depressing future of boring pleated skirts, comfort cardigans and sensible shoes! The secret of looking Contemporary or Currently Classic lies in the ability to see all the clues in the catwalk pictures and knowing how to introduce them subtly into your own wardrobe.

Study the catwalk pictures carefully – notice the predominant colours, the necklines, skirt lengths and jacket shapes, the types of fabric and patterns and, very importantly, the accessories, hair and make-up.

Each fashion season usually has about four 'themes' from which you can select different garments and accessories to update your look. At the time of writing there is a strong 'menswear/military' theme to fashion which was seen on the catwalks complete with combat hats, flying goggles, and bullet-lined belts! On pages 144 and 145, see how the Trendy woman incorporates a man's shirt, tie and belt with a maxi-length, fur-collared officer's coat; the Contemporary woman combines a short, leather military-style coat with military boots, but with classic skirt, scarf and ribbed tights; the Currently Classic woman merely buys a corduroy, naval reefer jacket to wear with a classic polo-neck sweater and trousers.

Another strong look as I write, particularly for evening wear, is based around a 'lingerie' theme. (See the illustrations on pages 146 and 147.) On the catwalk this caused shockwaves with completely see-through fabrics with no underwear beneath! In the illustration the Trendy woman wears the lingerie look with her undies prominently on display; the Contemporary woman chooses a bra-topped slip-dress with see-through over-dress; and the Currently Classic woman opts for a more discreet off-the-shoulder dress with one lingerie-style strap and side insets of lingerie-style lace. All three women look current, fashionable, modern – and young!

ACCESSORY STYLE

If you have a limited budget, hate clothes shopping, or simply prefer to have a wardrobe of completely classic, timeless clothes, it is possible to achieve a fashionable look simply by selecting a few new accessories each season. The classic 'little black dress' can look immediately up-to-date with the latest jewellery, bag and shoes (see pages 148 and 149). A classic blazer will suddenly look 'military' with a back-pack or with new, 'crested', metal buttons. A classic coat may just need the latest scarf, hat and gloves to re-vamp your image (see pages 150 and 151).

FASHION DIRECTIONS

The hard work of reading the catwalk clues can be done for you through my twice-yearly publication called *Fashion Directions*. Each season, I analyse all the latest themes, colours, accessories, hairstyles and cosmetic trends and present them in an easy-to-follow booklet to make your life easier.

Page 158 has details of how to order *Fashion Directions* as part of the complete 'Style Counsel Collection', containing your own personal style and colour guidelines, swatch of best colours and a quality lipstick.

Contemporary

Trendy

Currently Classic

Trendy

Currently Classic   Contemporary

Evening accessories

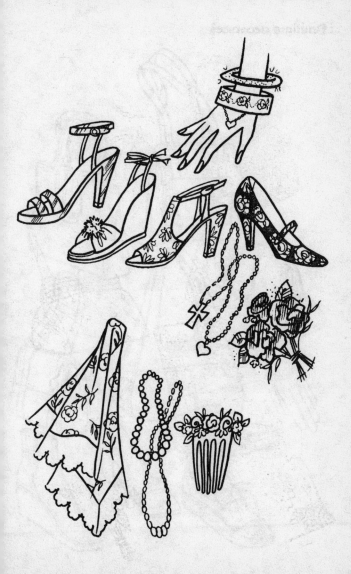

Daytime accessories

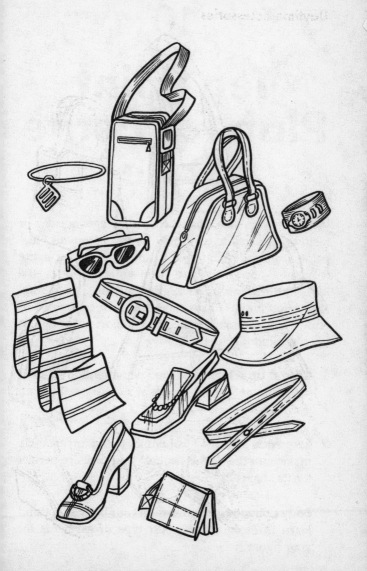

10

Ten Point Plan for Petite Style

Whatever your size, shape, colouring, age, lifestyle or fashion personality, you now have a complete blueprint to help develop your ultimate look as a petite woman. I hope you have been enlightened by the ideas outlined in this book – do send me your 'Before' and 'After' photos if you make any drastic changes! To end, I will summarise the most important points to bear in mind for the future.

1. **Keep It Up** – Remember to keep attention focused upwards, and avoid details which draw attention downwards.

2. **Face Facts** – As the focal point of your appearance, make sure the details around your face are perfect for its shape.

3. **Body Conscious** – Understand your body shape and learn to recognise the best type of garments for your figure.

4. **Slim Silhouette** – Aim to keep your profile as narrow as possible, especially when wearing longer styles.

5. **Balancing Act** – Always balance your accessories, patterns etc. with the scale of your body to avoid being overpowered.

6. **Vertical Vision** – Stress the vertical as much as possible in your outfits and avoid too many horizontal lines or breaks.

7. **Colour Directions** – Know your own Colour Direction and use it to select the shades for items around or on your face.

8. **Monochromatic Dressing** – Head-to-toe dressing in one shade will always make you look taller (deeper shades for fuller figures).

9. **Hang It All** – Rid your wardrobe of all clothes which are unflattering to your petite figure. Begin capsules for your lifestyle.

10. **Fashion Forever** – Keep up with fashion trends and accessories each season - lack of inches does not mean lack of style.

Have fun experimenting!

Index

Page numbers in *italic*
refer to the illustrations

accessories:
  beach accessories, 138
  and facial features,
    26–8, *29*
  scale, 64–7, *66*
  style, 143, *148–51*
angular accessories, 26–8,
  29
angular features, 26, *27*
ankles, thick, 58

bags, 67, 138, *148*, *150–1*
beach accessories, 138
blusher, 90–1, *91*
body:
  proportions, 47–62
  scale, 63–74, *64*, *68*, *73*
  shape, 31–46, *33–6*, *38*,

    40, *44–5*
bone size, 65
bottoms, large, 57, 135
Bright colour direction,
  80–1, 96
bust:
  large, 54, 132
  small, 55, 132–4, *133*

calves, thick, 58
capsule wardrobe, 105–6,
  108–25, 126–8
chin, double, 51
Classic style, 140–3, *145*,
  147
clothes, 98–128
  body shape, 31–46,
    33–6, *38*, *40*, *44–5*
  capsule wardrobe,
    105–6, *108–25*,
    126–8

colours, 48–9, 75–85
core pieces, 102–5,
   103–5
fabrics, 45–6
lifestyle analysis,
   99–100, *99*
style, 139–43, *144–7*
swimwear, 129–38
value for money, 100–1
wardrobe surgery,
   101–2
colour, 48–9, 75–85
   capsule wardrobe,
      105–6
   universal colours, 85
concealer, 89, *89*
Contemporary style,
   140–3, *144*, 147
Cool colour direction,
   83–4, 97
core clothes, 102–5, *103–5*
cosmetics, 86–97, *88–9*, *91*,
   93–4
curved accessories, 26–8,
   29
curved body, *35*
   capsule wardrobe,
      120–5
   clothes, *40*, *41*, *43*, *45*,
      46
curved features, 26, *27*

Deep colour direction,
   77–8, 95–6
diamond-shaped face, *21*,
   24, *24*
double chin, 51

evening accessories, *148–9*
eye-brows, 92
eyes:
   colours, 78–84
   glasses, 72
   make-up, 92, *93–4*

fabrics, 45–6
faces, 17–30
   and colours, 77
   cosmetics, 86–97, *88–9*,
      91, *93–4*
   features, 25–30, *27*
   shape, 18–25, *20–5*
Fashion Directions, 143
fashion personality, 140–3
features, facial, 25–30, *27*
figure, 31–46, *33–6*, *38*, *40*,
   44–5
flat-chested figure, 55
foundation, 87–8, *88*
fuller figure, swimwear,
   137–8

glasses, 28, 67, 70–2, *71*

hair:
  colours, 77–84
  styles, 69–70
hats, 18, 28, 67–70, *68*, 138
heart-shaped face, *20*, 23, *23*
hips, large, 57, 135

jewellery, and facial features, 26

large-scale accessories, 63–4, *65*, *66*
Lawson, Jacky, 11–12
legs:
  short, 59, 136–7, *136*
  thick calves/ankles, 58
lifestyle analysis, 99–100, *99*
Light colour direction, 78–9, 96
lipstick, 92–5

make-up, 86–97, *88–9*, *91*, *93–4*
medium-scale accessories, 64–5, *66*
midriff, 31
monochromatic dressing, 49

Muted colour direction, 81–2, 96–7

neck:
  long, 62
  short, 51
necklines, 28
noses, 72

oval face, *20*, 22, *22*

pear-shaped face, *20*, 23, *23*
personality, fashion, 140–3
Petite Clothing Co., 12
posture, 70
powder, 90
proportions, 47–62

rectangular face, *21*, 24, *24*
round face, *20*, 22, *22*

sandals, 138
scale, 63–74, *64*, *66*, *68*, *71*, *73*
scarves, 138
shoe size, 65
shoes, 72–4, *73*, 138, *149–51*

shoulders:
  broad, 52, 129–30, –
    130
  narrow, 53, 131, 131
skin colours, 78–84
sloping shoulders, 53
small-scale accessories,
  63–4, 65, 66
square face, 21, 24, 24
stomach, large, 57, 135
straight body, 33
  capsule wardrobe,
    108–13
  clothes, 36, 37, 42, 43,
    44, 46
style, 139–43, 144–7
sun hats, 138
swimwear, 129–38

tapered body, 34
  capsule wardrobe,
    114–19
  clothes, 38, 39, 43, 44,
    46
thighs, large, 57, 135
Trendy style, 140–2, 144,
  146

underwear, 46
universal colours, 85

waistline, 31–2
  short-waisted
    figure, 56, 134
wardrobe surgery, 101–2
Warm colour
  direction, 82–3, 97

FURTHER ADVICE FROM CAROL SPENSER

Carol Spenser will prepare for you your very own STYLE COUNSEL COLLECTION containing:

- Detailed analysis of your face and figure
- Solutions to your figure problems
- A flexible wardrobe plan for your lifestyle
- Hairstyle ideas for your face
- Colour suggestions for clothes and make-up
- A Swatch Wallet for near-face colours
- A quality lipstick selected for you
- *Fashion Directions* – current styles to suit your figure and colouring

For only **£29.95** – a saving of over £5.00 on the RRP of £35.00 (price includes p&p).

How do I apply?
You fill in a detailed questionnaire on your physical characteristics and fashion/colour preferences. Plus you send two recent colour photographs of yourself. Your form and photographs are analysed by Carol and her trained staff for your individual pack to be produced.

How does the cost compare?
A full colour and style consultation with an experienced reputable consultant ranges from £90 to £120 depending on where you live. Colour analysis alone can cost upwards of £50. *The Style Counsel Collection* is therefore one-third of the price of a total image consultation.

STYLE COUNSEL – Full Colour Book £12.99

If you would like further in-depth information on your best styles, colours and fashions, Carol Spenser's first book *Style Counsel* is indispensible. The full-colour photography throughout this stunning book brings all her concepts and advice beautifully to life.

REPLY SLIP

Please send me _____ copies of *Style Counsel* at £12.99 each

Please send me _____ applications for the *Style Counsel Collection* at £29.95 each

I enclose a cheque/postal order for £ _____ (payable to Public Persona Ltd)

I wish to pay by Access / Visa / Mastercard

Card No. _____

Expiry date _____ Signature _____

Name _____

Address _____

_____ Post code _____

Simply cut out or copy this slip to place your order, or telephone the credit card hotline on 01223 812737 or fax 01223 812853.

Return your completed slip to:
Public Persona Ltd, The Vineyards,129 High Street, Bottisham, Cambridge CB5 9BA England

E. Mail: publicpersona@dial.pipex.com